Minimalism

Beginners Guide to Minimalism

Nia Asha

Table of Contents

Book Description

Is your life cluttered, overly-busy and filled with time-consuming chores that don't make you happy? Adopting a minimalist approach to your life will change the way you live it!

In today's consumer-driven society, 'things' have replaced people. We work hard to possess the very things that consume our time, and make our lives feel empty and meaningless. Another way exists, that focuses on eliminating the physical, mental and emotional clutter in your average day.

In *Minimalism*, I'll take you through a total overhaul of your current lifestyle, habits and mindset. You will discover that by switching to minimalism, you'll make room for the things in life you've been missing – love, family, free time and reconnecting with who you are, and what you want.

In this book you'll discover:

- The main reasons why people switch to a minimalist lifestyle

- How to declutter your space like a minimalist pro

- Where to start when decluttering your social life

- Applying minimalism to your finances for better results

- How minimalism impacts your mind and becomes a core habit

- The main lessons that minimalism teaches us about a happy life

It's been a long time since you reassessed what you do, and what you have. Minimalism will free you from the endless barrage of wanting, FOMO and inadequacy the consumerist system inspires.

You have the power to change how you live your life. Bring it all back to what matters and throw away the rest! Return to a simpler, happier way of enjoying how you live.

Discover the practice of minimalism with this step-by-step guide.

Buy it now to learn how!

Introduction

What is Minimalism?

Minimalism is the processes of scaling back from having too much to having just enough. People take on minimalism because they want freedom from things in their lives. Be it material possessions, toxic relationships or mental clutter; minimalism has become the go-to lifestyle for more millennials today. It is not a lifestyle that caters for the youth; any person despite the age can adopt the practice in their life. Even if minimalism advocates for having fewer things, that doesn't mean that material possession is bad. The idea here is to have the things that one needs and appreciates in their life today. Keeping things that no longer serve you or buying stuff because of a scarcity mentality is highly discouraged.

The reason this lifestyle is gaining popularity is that more and more people are starting to realize the value we attach to items. The fact that most of us cannot separate our memories and emotions from material things is alarming. The amount of consumerism in the world is also at an all-time high. People have always loved things but not as much as they do now that there is so much access thanks to technology.

Minimalism allows someone to make their list of things they need to keep. You may still retain most of the stuff you have if you decide that you need them. No two people can have the same wants or needs. Whatever you think is trash could be relevant to someone else. The guiding principle here is to look within yourself and make a deliberate, conscious decision on what you want to keep or throw away.

For anyone that is wondering if this lifestyle is for them, they need to ask themselves a few questions. Would I benefit from scaling down? Do I attach so much value to material possessions? Am I holding on to baggage that I need to let go? I am not saying that these are the only questions there are to be asked? Every person is attracted to the lifestyle because of different reasons. But they only become true minimalists if when they are free to focus on what they deem essential. People are in constant pursuit of happiness, true freedom and a fulfilled existence. And to that conclusion, there cannot be a shortcut.

For any beginner starting something new can be daunting especially if it involves making life-changing decisions. As there are no shortcuts, there are also no set guidelines on how to achieve true minimalism status. The first step towards starting the journey can be the hardest, but it can very well be the best decision you make in your life. Maintaining the lifestyle after you have already started can also be a struggle, but it should not deter you from your final goal. Anything worth having is not easy to get.

Before embarking on this wild ride, look for success stories for inspiration and pick some of the things they learned in their journey. Otto von Bismarck said, "Only fools learn from experience." Because of the internet, there is no need to start from the ground up. Learn from other people but also realize that you are going to make your own mistakes. Own them, don't dwell on them and eventually move on. This whole process is an individual journey that one needs to take alone so that they can gain what they truly want.

Even when someone has become a successful minimalist for a few years, the basic principles still apply. Keep questioning the things you own. Evaluate your relationships often to see if they still need your presence. One doesn't just give up this lifestyle when things start improving in their life. You will always have to grow and evolve to lead a better life.

Chapter 1: Minimalism Today

"Less is more." - Mies Van Der Rohe. 1886.

Why is Minimalism Important? Is it Just a Trend?

Most of society today is under the impression that living a minimalist lifestyle means letting go of something physical. On the contrary, giving away your material possession is not all that minimalism is about. Minimalism is cutting out what is unnecessary in life, be it frivolous expenditure, meaningless social interactions or general negativity. Minimalism is about happiness in one's life and not about success. There is a time at when feels like fulfillment seems out of reach.

Minimalism may be able to chart out what areas of life are not at their best. Sometimes we are led to believe that specific things, usually physical belongings and property are the measures of happiness and contentment. This is a very negative way of going about life. We are led to believe that settling down and slowing down the adventurous spirit is what a mature person does, that taking care of one's responsibilities is what an adult is expected to do. But this is not entirely true. You can't just live your life paying bills and surviving. Going through life doing only what is expected is not the way to be a well-rounded human being. One must leave time to work on their mentality, platonic and romantic relationships and pursuing what is of benefit to your life.

Minimalism is now a trend that has been growing steadily over the years. It is believed to have roots within the Scandinavian people in Europe. The digital generation, the millennials have however popularized it. Most millennials have slowly realized that the economy is not what it used to be and are determined to live within their means. This has led to the adaptation of this less clustered way of life. Millennials are the group that has contributed to social and environmental awareness on the benefits of minimalism. Minimalism seeks to address consumerism and environmental issues using its philosophy of living with less. This trend is not just a trending hashtag on social media; it is a powerful movement that if adopted by everybody could change the world.

As we live in a consumerist society today, people have placed an unwarranted importance on material things and trends to maintain a false sense of importance and success. The age of the internet has given room for the rise of negativity and a shallow way of thinking. In this regard, keeping up with trends has led to the accumulation of many things, collections of makeup and closets filled with things that go out style within months. As minimalism is a journey, it helps to start by taking stock of the physical characteristics that are taking up space in our homes and removing them, opening up space for tranquility, because if you cannot feel peaceful in your own home, there is little point to the evaluation. We focus too much on the economy instead of looking at intrinsic values.

Reasons to Pursue Minimalism

As for the reasons to pursue a minimalist lifestyle, there are many, differing from person to person.

- One may include achieving goals sooner; Minimalists are more determined when pursuing their goals in school or life which is a positive impact of minimalism.

- Minimalists tend to stay away from television and social media. Their phones and computers are usually for work and occasional connection with friends and family. The space that would otherwise be used to mull over the internet will be free to be used more productively.

- Minimalists are calmer, having decluttered their minds of negativity. They have more peaceful thoughts and can be instrumental in deflating an explosive interaction and aid in mending broken relationships.

- By avoiding social media, a minimalist has more time for interpersonal relationships, particularly romantic relationships. You become more open when you spend quality time with your partner and you get to learn more about them.

- Minimalism allows an individual to opt out of options that will lead to debt. Less spending decreases the need for credit and smaller housing leads to fewer bills and mortgage costs are reduced significantly.

- Less time being worried about their own life allows a minimalist to see other people — their strengths, struggles, hardships and more. And with a more evolved emotional state, they can put themselves in other's shoes and assist where they can and reach out for encouragement.

- Minimalists can discover their purpose faster than other modern individuals. Having cut down on screen time and gone out into the world to see and experience what others have to offer as well as establishing strong interpersonal relationships, they can fulfill their lives and encourage and assist others reach the same level of fulfillment.

- Developing healthy friendships is essential to a minimalist. Having been able to discover who they are, they seek to make connections with people who can build on that while getting rid of those who seem to leech off of them. However, they also tend to maintain old friendships that persevered during hard times.

- Minimalists can utilize the little they have to fulfill their lives. They can overcome where others cannot see a way out.

- They can grow their talents to improve their own lives as well as that of others.

- Traveling is a breeze for minimalists. They tend to pack light and pick up what they need along the way. Their joy is not in what can be used to remember the visit but in the experiences themselves.

- They are punctual and tend to maintain good rapport with authority figures who can assist in their pursuit of accomplishment. Deadlines and appointments are adhered to religiously.

- Minimalists are less likely to fear failure as they are more confident in their abilities and have built rapport and gathered necessary connections through good relationships to see their vision accomplished.

- Having a clear mind allows minimalists to be less stressed.

- They tend to be empathetic. Being more involved in personal allows people to come to you with problems, and being a present friend, they are always willing to listen. This builds their friends trust and value.

- Minimalists tend to make friends faster. Their positivity attracts new people toward them and their willingness to be involved and engaged in the relationship keeps people interested.

- Minimalists tend to have a keen eye on the things that they need. Ridding their homes of clutter allows them to see what they need and can decide to get it based on this assessment.

- They are more innovative and can enter the entrepreneurship industry unhindered. Their confidence allows them to face the risks of starting a new venture and maximize their profits.

- Cutting back on unhealthy habits and finding time to exercise they can stay fit and healthy.

- They understand that it's the little things in life that bring the most happiness.

- Family relationships are meaningful, just as friends and romantic partners are. More time is made to grow these relationships, strengthen the bonds and spread to love to the younger generations.

- By building rapport among their professional colleagues, they can earn respect based off of their hard work and determination. They also assist those who are struggling to achieve their goals.

- Minimalism allows for a lot freer time which is one's to do with as they please. A lot of this is reinvested in work, relationships or adventure.

- For those who are environmentally conscious, there is no better way to live as you preach than to practice minimalism.

Understanding Minimalism

Minimalism may be an ongoing trend, with most people laughing it off as a fad that will be discarded as quickly as it was adopted, but there are clear benefits to decluttering your life. Most of these range from health to social and even your finances will thank you for this change. Of all the benefits that minimalism has to offer, mental benefits are more prominent. Their focus is increased exponentially when you are not always worrying about all the distractions that would be taking place otherwise. Productivity will shoot through the roof, and your work will be grateful for it. There can be much more to be accomplished by a focused mind.

Peace is achieved through both physical decluttering and mental decluttering. Tuning out the external noise allows one to be stress-free, enabling one to avoid triggers caused by triggering sensory organs. Avoiding stress enables one to avoid the numerous health conditions associated with it.

Once taking up a minimalist life, one can clearly define what it is they want and what it is they need. Cutting back on spending to achieve happiness allows for financial freedom enjoyable experiences. Sparing money with these kinds of purchases can allow one to travel and experience something they otherwise would not have been able to. Skip the presents on special occasions and opt instead for making unforgettable memories with people you love.

The increase in consumerism has negatively affected the environment, and climate change is evident. The more we buy, the greater the impact. A lot of what we buy impulsively or because it is rarely used and ultimately thrown out. Even the way these products are packaged is a cause for concern. Plastic is used for this, from packing materials from goods bought online to the containers in which take away food is delivered. Plastic is non-biodegradable, and that is a massive problem for the environment. The industries that manufacture these products need water, which is depleting the water reserves we have. They emit 60% of the greenhouse gases that are depleting the ozone layer. Companies are starting to feel the weight of production cost and are now using cheaper, readily available materials, which is causing cheap productions to flood the market. Minimalists tend to go for higher quality products which lasts longer thus reducing waste. They live in smaller homes which reduce energy consumption for light and heat. A minimalist uses fewer cleaning supplies. They spend less on home repairs and are virtually incapable of overconsumption, and they don't have space!

There are types of minimalists. There are three different ways in which minimalists wish to practice their lifestyle but follow the same simple foundation of a lifestyle centered on less.

- The aesthetic minimalist – they tend to care about aesthetics. It is not that they have less, but they indeed display very little of it. They tend to go for the simplest things, dull color, simple design, simple textures, and the likes.

- Essential minimalists – they like to challenge themselves to see how little they can survive off of. They buy less, use less and have only the most basic of requirements. They do not like to waste, so they will buy the best quality they can afford. If they can have only one thing, it should be the best.

- Experiential minimalists – these are the ones who seek adventure above everything else. They own very little just because they move around a lot and not because they had to throw things out. They are sometimes called "backpack" minimalist and are likely to want to learn new skills.

- Sustainable minimalists – they love the environment and are focused on cutting back things that bring harm to the environment. They will keep a lot of what is important if it means they don't have to go out and buy it. They aspire to live as green as is possible while making do. They will probably learn how to make what they need from scratch.

- Thrifty minimalists – they known as the sustainable types, but their goal is to spend as little as possible. They thrift for clothes and equipment and might even grow their food. They love tools that can multitask and will sometimes live with someone else to save rent. They can, however, be prone to holding on to things they consider important, so they don't have to buy it in the future.

- Mindful minimalists – they tend to use decluttering as a spiritual experience. They get rid of unnecessary things to let go of negative emotions like guilt or stress. It allows them to find inner peace and become better. They may read about spiritual decluttering.

For anyone looking to become a minimalist, there are a few suggestions on where to start. You can write down what it is you want to achieve by becoming a minimalist. They can serve as inspiration for when things get too tricky. They will help you stick to your transition. Get rid of anything you do not use or if you have a duplicate, toss it out too. Sometimes a simple technique helps to declutter. Put everything you don't need in a box and put it away for 30 days. If at the end of the month you don't remember what was in the box or didn't take anything out, give it away. Traveling light is another step. Try packing for two days if you are going away for four. If you need something, you will improvise. Gradually you will become more comfortable with traveling light. Try finding items of clothing that can be mixed and matched to create different looks thus decreasing your closet size. It has been known to make life easier. Try eating the same thing for each meal for a week. Rotate the choices and see how you like it. This goes a long way in making decisions about food. If you have ever found yourself needing money for an emergency, then you know how stressful it can be. Try setting a small amount of money as a savings goal. Save a little cash.

Even if you are paying back a debt, do this anyway. When the goal is reached, you will have extra cash for a rainy day, and you will not be stressed about it.

All in all, minimalism allows one to promote what is important to them while removing other distractions. It seeks to avoid consumerism and eliminates the need to possess. Modern life is fast-paced and in that there is little chance to connect. And in a world that holds up a specific lifestyle as the gold standard, it is minimalism that provides an alternative way of living, a healthier way of living. Minimalists make a personal choice to live in this way. After achieving a minimalistic exterior, it allows for space to declutter the interior of our lives. Minimalism is accepted worldwide as a way of life, and there are quite some people who have successfully made the transition from modern life to a more subdued minimalist lifestyle.

Chapter 2: Taking Stock

"Any half-awake materialist well knows – that which you hold holds you." - Tom Robbins. 1936.

Possessions and Life

Human beings can be blinded to believe that they need material things to be happy. They love to accumulate physical possessions. From ancient civilization, the property has been ingrained into society taking up different roles. Some believed wealth meant blessing and favor from the gods. Others thought that property was only intended to be held by royalty. Despite whatever belief we have about ownership, it is clear that wealth is used to symbolize our status in society. These items are used to signal who we are and where we belong in society to ourselves and others. Even after death, an individual's accomplishments and wealth are regarded as a legacy. It is almost impossible to separate oneself from ownership completely, and it is after all our nature as human beings.

Even at a young age, we are aware of the idea that it is possible to possess something and claim it as your own. We became attached to specific toys or blankets and would cry at the thought of it being taken away or destroyed. There have even been instances of possessiveness in young children who are asked to share with others, and others have burst into a violent rage when this special object is taken away and given to someone else. We even experienced jealousy when we saw someone with something better, something we wanted. As teenagers, we started to use objects we possessed as indicators of who we are. We personalized school bags and jackets to act as an expression of our personalities. In adulthood, these belongings cease to be just inanimate objects, and they become part of whom we are or who we hope to become.

Sometimes possessions are used to convey specific attributes about ourselves. For courtship, men tend to wear expensive watches and name brand clothes to signal availability and status. We use certain brands to show we belong to a unique club or movement. Exclusivity is a further indicator of status. Society has instilled the notion of the more property you have in your name means you are successful. People end up scrambling to collect as much as they can and end up having a lot of useless junk. However, people also gather things out of sentiment. Sometimes we want to close one chapter of our lives and start fresh such as the case of marriage, moving to a new home and leaving school. Even after death, people's belongings are left behind to give comfort to those they have left behind. Even with objects, we would not regularly use, we attach a memory of the deceased, and it is like they are still alive and end up having a lot of useless junk. However, people also collect things out of sentiment. Loss of our possessions may be traumatizing, as over the time we have had them they become precious. It may be equated to the feeling of losing someone close to us.

Property is not only crucial among, individuals but groups as well. More than just identity, the value associated with property belonging to particular groups increases. If a house belonged to a grandparent, members of the extended family would want to keep it in the family and use it as a place for family gatherings and thus strengthen the familial bond. Objects with important historical significance say to a country, or a particular community will be cherished and displayed for the members of the public who belong to the community to enjoy. Property like this is usually protected to a greater extent by law and finance to preserve them. Even if they end up being put up for sale their value is increased to make up for their historical significance.

Why Keep So Many Things We Don't need?

This is commonly referred to as hoarding, and it is the inability to discard belongings regardless of their value. This is not to be confused with collecting. Collectors are proud of their collections and enjoy talking about them as well as spend money and time caring for and adding to the collection while hoarders just do not put that much effort into their possessions and are often embarrassed by their items even after acquiring new ones. Some cases of hoarding have been so extreme to the point of where legal action has had to be taken against the hoarder.

Most cases of hoarding are not as extreme and usually involve a lot of clutter. There are many reasons why people hoard. For some, it is a matter of a psychological disorder. Most cases have been linked to obsessive-compulsive personality disorder (OCPD), obsessive-compulsive personality disorder (OCD), attention-deficit/hyperactivity disorder (ADHD) and depression. Others feel these items will become useful and are stored like this for a rainy day. This can be attributed to anxiety over being unprepared. Others place sentimental value on these objects while also believing they are unique or irreplaceable. Some attach memories, assuming they would not be able to remember a particular experience or person that is tied to the item in question. Others like to say that they are saving these items for a celebration or a time when they have earned them. In the case of clothes, they hang on to them with the hope that one day they will lose weight and fit into that smaller size. Either way, none of these reasons is well founded, and help is required to be able to let go of the clutter.

The Psychological Impact of Hoarding

Hoarding comes from a place of severe mental instability. Instead of leading an emotionally peaceful and positive life, a hoarder has to deal with the parts of their braid that feel pain and conflict experiencing even more turmoil. They have put themselves in a position that leaves them feeling constant psychological pain.

Lack of concentration is common amongst hoarders. Most people find it hard to be productive around any mess. The clutter overloads your sense and leaves you feeling restless and stressed.

Hoarding increases stress levels. As a hoarder tries to deal with the clutter, their brain starts to think it is multitasking and releases stress hormones. Instead of being able to focus on one thing, the mind is overwhelmed by everything that is happening and sends a signal of surrender.

Hoarding does not only affect the individual. Their families and other relationships suffer as well. It leads to conflicts within the family unit. Common arguments include arguing over finances, with the hoarder compulsively buying things to feed their habit and adding more storage for them, conflicts over space, conflict over barred areas in the house that are being used as storage for the hoarder and loss of trust if the family attempts to clean these areas.

Children suffer poor development and social lives due to health problems that are likely to occur in an unkempt house, as well as the embarrassment they would feel after inviting their friends over and are discovered to be living in filth. The parent might also forbid them from asking friends over due to their embarrassment. The children might develop resentment toward the parent whose lifestyle is causing their minimal social interactions. They may also become conflicted over whom to choose in an argument, the parent who hoards or the one who does not. If a neighbor catches wind of the situation, they may feel inclined to inform the authorities, and the children might be taken away from their parents on the grounds or child endangerment.

Even in adulthood, children of hoarders still experience the effects. Their relationship with the parent who hoards is strained and may also prevent their children from being around their grandparents. This drives a wedge between the family and isolates the hoarder even more. They may blame the parents for any psychological issues they developed as a child living with them. This includes "caregiver burden" which leaves them feeling chronically worried and suffering from anxiety and an inability to cope after having to take care of the parent. This may lead to them developing other issues like lack of self-esteem and difficulty planning for their future.

Spouses to hoarders can end up feeling resentment and hostile towards their spouse after putting up with their lifestyle for a long time. This usually ends in separation or divorce which further breaks apart the family. This affects the children's upbringing and general well-being of everyone involved.

Beyond the psychological impacts, there are safety concerns within the homes of hoarders. A hoarder rarely cleans and does not allow his belongings to be touched, or get affected by dust, pollen, grease, animal fur and spilled liquids that lead to mildew and fungi as well as pests. Family members with allergies will find it difficult to stay in the house. Headaches, asthma and breathing problems will be common in the household.

Usually, there is so much clutter in the house that it becomes near impossible to move around. Piles of clutter have to be moved to create room for movement. This could prove dangerous as piles of clutter can fall and cause injury. Some hoarders even keep hazardous items in the home such as swords or mousetraps.

There is a real threat of fire with the clutter. Many of these items are made of wood, paper, and flammable materials being stored close to stoves and heaters among other sources of fire. And with all the things in the way, the event of an accidental fire could prove fatal because reaching fire extinguishers and exits will be difficult with everything in the way.

There have been reports of floors caving under the weight of everything stored in the house. If this were to occur while the house is occupied, severe injuries and even death could happen.

There are methods for coping with hoarding. Admitting that they are hoarding is difficult, but it is the first step to recovery. It is essential that they choose to seek help. Change cannot be forced upon them. Once this decision is made, seeking psychological help is the next step. See a psychiatrist and get to the root of the problem and learn new techniques that will help them cope with their emotions. Family and friends should express how the hoarding has affected their lives but remain supportive and figure out a way to bond if the hoarder is to recover. Encourage and uplift them so that they do not slink back into their cocoon of depression and lead to a relapse.

The Value Placed on Property

We previously discussed how sentiment is set on certain objects even when they hold no use. For example, the son of a recently deceased parent may hold on to music records they would listen to in their youth, despite not owning a record player because they are outdated and have become rare, even if they wanted to go out and get one, it would prove difficult. A gift bestowed upon us by a friend or romantic partner may be kept to remind ourselves of fond memories that they associate with the item. Parents will leave their children's belongings untouched, long after they move, out to remember a time when they were utterly dependent on their parents

But how do we measure the value of our property? Is it in how sentimental it is, where it came from or who gave it to us? Did it belong to someone we loved or idolized like a role model? Is it the period in which an item is in our possession? Or the amount of time and money spent to acquire it? Things like houses or cars cost money and time to obtain and maintain and hold enough value to justify getting them insured. Items inherited from deceased loved ones and role models are irreplaceable and unique.

So how can we tell when we truly care about something? We care for them a great deal by cleaning and grooming, refurbishing old furniture, home repairs, having our cars serviced and insurance against loss and damage. This much we do for our physical possessions.

Materialism is not a bad thing. Think about what your motivations to accumulate these possessions are. When used to improve one's well-being as well as that of others this is wholly justified while extending what is favorable within ourselves in acquiring property. People are motivated by greed and power, and their need to purchase property is therefore selfish.

Despite how much we want to keep our belongings, it soon becomes overwhelming. It's now time to let go. Start checking for things that are no longer useful. Maybe they were in use for a long time, but you found a cheaper or simpler alternative. Get rid of anything you don't use or wouldn't buy any more. You obviously would not want to toss out anything you love, but keeping everything is no longer an option. Remove everything that does not hold any sentiment. If you have gifts that you didn't care for, you can put them all together and give them away. Sure enough, there is someone who will appreciate them more. Never allow your space to have duplicates when it is so much harder to get rid of sentimental clutter more than anything else. It is usually guilt that makes people hold on to sentimental things, not love or nostalgia. Don't let the guilt associated with the item keep you from getting rid of it. You can also pass these items on to other people who would be willing to keep it. That way it is never truly gone. Look for things you can reuse and recycle. Don't let everything go to waste when it could be transformed into something you truly need. Papers, pictures and other small objects could be turned in to a scrapbook. This is an excellent way of saving space and getting to keep little trinkets that are valuable to you. Keep in mind that as earlier discussed, there is no need to throw everything out, only what is unnecessary.

Chapter 3: Decluttering Your Space

"One can furnish a room very luxuriously by taking out furniture rather than putting it in." - Francis Jourdain. 1876.

Messy spaces contribute to disorganized thoughts, lack of focus and general laxity in life. When there is clutter everywhere around us, we tend to be uninspired and unproductive. There is a need to declutter to remove the negative energy associated with the disorder in your surroundings. Decluttering has been known to be therapeutic to those who practice it.

A Step by Step Guide to Decluttering

Now that we know the impact of being in a disorganized environment let us begin to declutter.

The first thing to do should be to figure out where to put papers and documents. Paper accounts for a lot of the clutter in the home. Pick a box or a container that will hold the documents as you collect them. This makes it easier to sort them later and ensures nothing gets lost along the way.

Start small. Pick a small portion in a room and start clearing it. Make sure not to put anything in this area unless it belongs there or is being used. Keep going until the whole house is covered.

Pick a surface. It could be a shelf or a countertop. Clear out what is unnecessary and leave only what is essential to the surface like a flower vase or a book that you read a lot.

Schedule time for decluttering. A lot of the time people are busy with work or school and don't have time to stay at home and clean the house. Pick a weekend or anytime you have time off and declutter your home. Get your family and friends involved as well. This will make the process fun and will help make significant progress if you are unable to finish by the end of the break. You could finish on your own.

Finding places for things you regularly use is a great help. These are items you constantly reach for but never seem to have any place to put them. Walk around the house and find it easy to reach spots where you can put them. As you find places for other things in the home, you will notice the house start to clear up and finding spaces for things you don't use will become easier.

Cables in the home keep piling up. Nowadays every home has multiple electronic devices which come with their cables. Eventually, these cables accumulate and become an eye-sore and detangling them becomes a nightmare. You can sort all the wires that go into the same device and tie them together using zip-ties or black tape.

Before you begin the decluttering process, take a step back and visualize where you would like everything to go once you are done with the process. This gives you a guide and saves on time that would have been spent during trying to decide where everything goes. It also helps to get rid of what does not belong and free up much-needed space.

Sometimes there are things you're not sure whether to keep or donate. Put these things aside for some time. Mark your calendar, so you remember to check on it. Usually, there is nothing of utmost importance and if there is you can take it out. The rest you can put out.

Decluttering gives a perfect opportunity to donate. Cleaning your home reveals old clothes that you do not wear and ones that do not fit anymore among other things like toys and extra dishes. Donating them to the needy allows us to do our part in society to make life better for others less fortunate than we are.

Make a list before you make a purchase. This is only for non-essential goods like electronics, clothes, and accessories. Keep the list for an about a month. If you still want to buy something on that list, get it. Usually, you will find that the urge to buy these items disappears within the month. This method helps to control the accumulation of unnecessary things and saves money by cutting back on impulse buying.

Teach yourself and your kids, roommates and significant others the habit of cleaning up after themselves. This reduces the amount of clutter that accumulates over time. Keep up this habit up until you're used to it.

Every time you bring home something new, take something else out in its place. It usually is the thing you're replacing it with, or it could be something of a similar size or bigger. This controls clutter.

Have folder or files to store paperwork in so that they do not get in the way. Have extras in case you need to create a new category.

Every time you are organizing paperwork, make decisions on how to deal with them quickly. File them in the assigned file or throw them away if they are of no use. If you can't decide on what to do on the spot, make a note and place the papers in a file for later action. Never put back the papers in the original pile; it will undo all your hard work.

If you spot something you no longer use as you are going about the house, place it in a box and throw it out or give it away. This works for clothes, notebooks, accessories, and even kitchen equipment. This will help declutter the house slowly until everything left has a purpose.

Check the medicine cabinet and drawers. A lot of items in these places are either not being used or completely forgotten about. Take everything out and start sorting them out into piles. Everything you need goes back in into the drawers and cabinet. Empties and expired products get thrown out, and unused products get donated.

Enjoy the fruits of your labor. Sit back and appreciate how good everything looks now that it is organized. Keep your home looking clean, and you will experience a change in your general outlook, like increased confidence and general productivity.

Changing Your Décor and Aesthetic to a Minimalistic Look

To enhance your newly decluttered space, switching to a minimalistic aesthetic for your space is a good idea. Minimalistic décor allows you to keep your home organized as there isn't that much in the home. This look may seem simple enough to achieve, but it can be quite tricky.

The first step is to come up with a base color. It is advisable to pick a laid-back color, usually related to white. This is because it inspires serenity and calm. This does not mean that it has to be boring. You can add a little color, but make sure it can blend with more earth-tone colors and tans. Then comes the decision of what to put in the room. With the neutral base, choosing what goes with it is harder than it appears. Everything seems appropriate enough. Make sure to pick things that everyone would like. Go for quality items. If you have a limited number of items you can add to the space, make it the best. The environment will thank you.

The empty space provided by this look allows you to play around and create a focal point. Clearing surfaces give you the opportunity to edit what you display in the limited space. Only go for simple things. Scatter two or three photographs in the space and add a flower vase. Remember not to go overboard.

If you still think that the space could stand to be livelier, pick a statement piece and put it on an empty wall. This could be anything that stands out depending on your taste. It could work to break the ice if you have company over.

To make the space more interesting, you can add textures in similar tones. You could also pick items that are of the same color but different hues. Adding a pattern could make things more fun. Introduce colors that would naturally go together.

Pick a simple, stylish storage option. It contributes to the chic aesthetic while keeping your stuff hidden away. You could always refurbish something old you had to make it match the aesthetic of the rest of the home and use it the same way.

Use natural light. Try your hardest not to obstruct the light that comes into your space. Use thin or sheer curtain material or blinds for privacy but leave the windows uncovered if you can.

Use clean lines and soft edges. Keeping with the theme of simplicity, make sure your accessories, light fixtures, and cabinet handles have simple designs. Flat surfaces are encouraged and should be left open.

Switch to minimalist décor keeps the home decluttered by getting rid of unnecessary things in the house. Clutter does not need to be the junk on the floor. When we have too much going on in the space regarding décor, it can disrupt the flow of the aesthetic and overload the senses.

Can Minimalism Be Integrated into Family Life?

Minimalism is a growing trend and is becoming a more acceptable way of life. It insists on less is more. The less you have to deal with, the more time and space you have for other important aspects of your life. While minimalism is considered a personal lifestyle choice, parents or caregivers can incorporate this into their families and improve their lives as well.

There are many reasons why minimalism should be incorporated within families. The health and psychological benefits of switching to a minimalist life are numerous; it is generally easier to live like a minimalist among other reasons. It should be noted that making the transition to minimalism as a family could be difficult since we are dealing with different people who have different needs.

As a minimalist, you might want your family to join in on the freeing experience but are not sure how. Start by decluttering what belongs to you without pressuring anyone else to purge.

The journey to becoming a minimalist family should begin with evaluating what is important as a family and determining what to get rid of and what to keep. Start as an experiment and push forward from there, kids love to be involved in family activities without having to learn that their lifestyles are about to change. Remove distractions from your routine so that you can focus on improving your lifestyle. Make sure you do not neglect their needs on account of this change. Showing your usual levels of affection and then some may persuade them to join your cause. Avoid judging what everyone else has and do not put pressure on them to change right away; it will just leave them feeling annoyed and misunderstood. Don't keep them in the dark about what you are doing. Take the time to explain what you are doing and let them know of the benefits. Use examples with the kids so they can understand. Help them understand that what you are doing can help others who are in need and appeal to their compassion. Overall don't go through this alone and risk them thinking that you are slowly losing your mind. You risk giving them reasons to fight you on the change. They will find their way as opposed to you telling them what to do.

To begin the transition, start by taking account of everything your possessions and daily routines. Cut out everything that is of no value or wastes time. Keep what is special and brings your family closer like traditions or games. Make a list or a board and hang it up to motivate the other members to stay on course. Cutting out the time and space wasters is very rewarding. Saving time otherwise spent on tv or video games saves time for something more important. Donating unused toys and clothes clears up space and declutters the home. These three areas do not involve a lot of emotional soul searching or emotional investment and are therefore the easiest to knock down from the list. Don't think about organizing. The goal of the transition is not to organize but to remove unnecessary things in life to free up time for other interests. Schedule these activities; otherwise, they become forgotten. Cut off spending if it is not for food and other basics.

For the children, getting them involved ensures they learn early on and can transition gradually. Start by setting an example. They should see you do the same things you require them to do. Make sure you also give clear instructions so that they know what to do. Establish the practice of donation by encouraging them to give away what they don't want or need. Set up a specific spot for donation the house. Have the kids sort their items into categories, that way they interact with each thing to see if they still want to keep. Set up limits for their stuff, so they don't accumulate things they don't need. If they share a room, have them designate areas where they can display their belongings. When space runs out, they are forced to take away things they don't need.

Minimalism doesn't need to be about getting rid of only physical belongings. It does, however, help to be grateful and appreciative for the things we do own. It also makes the goals of the family clearer, and the parents can confidently make decisions that affect the family.

At this point there is a lot of free time cleared up that can be used for family bonding and travel. These activities that families participate in together build the relationship. Going through this transition as a family is rewarding, and for the children, they can take these lessons into adulthood. With patience and determination, it is indeed possible to find a system that works for everyone.

Add more storage for them, conflicts over space, conflict over barred areas in the house that are being used as storage for the hoarder and loss of trust if the family attempts to clean these areas.

Children suffer poor development and social lives due to health problems that are likely to occur in an unkempt house, as well as the embarrassment they would feel after inviting their friends over and are discovered to be living in filth. The parent might also forbid them from asking friends over due to their embarrassment. The children might develop resentment toward the parent whose lifestyle is causing their minimal social interactions. They may also become conflicted over whom to choose in an argument, the parent who hoards or the one who does not. If a neighbor catches wind of the situation, they may feel inclined to inform the authorities, and the children might be taken away from their parents on the grounds or child endangerment.

Even in adulthood, children of hoarders still experience the effects. Their relationship with the parent who hoards is strained and may also prevent their children from being around their grandparents. This drives a wedge between the family and isolates the hoarder even more. They may blame the parents for any psychological issues they developed as a child living with them. This includes "caregiver burden" which leaves them feeling chronically worried and suffering from anxiety and an inability to cope after having to take care of the parent. This may lead to them developing other issues like lack of self-esteem and difficulty planning for their future.

Spouses to hoarders can end up feeling resentment and hostile towards their spouse after putting up with their lifestyle for a long time. This usually ends in separation or divorce which further breaks apart the family. This affects the children's upbringing and general well-being of everyone involved.

Beyond the psychological impacts, there are safety concerns within the homes of hoarders. Since the hoarder rarely cleans and does not allow his belongings to be touched, dust, pollen, grease, animal fur and spilled liquids that lead to mildew and fungi as well as pests. Family members with allergies will find it difficult to stay in the house. Headaches, asthma and breathing problems will be common in the household.

Usually, there is so much clutter in the house that it becomes near impossible to move around. Piles of clutter have to be moved to create room for movement. This could prove dangerous as piles of clutter can fall and cause injury. Some hoarders even keep hazardous items in the home such as swords or mousetraps.

There is a real threat of fire with the clutter. Many of these items are made of wood, paper, and flammable materials being stored close to stoves and heaters among other sources of fire. And with all the things in the way, the event of an accidental fire could prove fatal because reaching fire extinguishers and exits will be difficult with everything in the way.

There have been reports of floors caving under the weight of everything stored in the house. If this were to occur while the house is occupied, severe injuries and even death could happen.

There are methods for coping with hoarding. Admitting that they are hoarding is difficult, but it is the first step to recovery. It is essential that they choose to seek help. Change cannot be forced upon them. Once this decision is made, seeking psychological help is the next step. See a psychiatrist and get to the root of the problem and learn new techniques that will help them cope with their emotions. Family and friends should express how the hoarding has affected their lives but remain supportive and figure out a way to bond if the hoarder is to recover. Encourage and uplift them so that they do not slink back into their cocoon of depression and lead to a relapse.

Chapter 4: Relationships

"Collect moments, not things." — Paulo Coelho.

Humans are social beings; they need to form relationships with the people around them. The need to connect with other people is something we are born with; it is psychological. Whether those relationships are fulfilling, however, that is entirely up to us. When we are young, the relationships that are most important to us are those with family and friends and peers. Once we reach adolescence, we start to explore relationships outside the family unit in seeking independence from our parents, bonding further with peers and discovering romance. Young adults find themselves thrust into new environments and begin cultivating modern lifestyles and reaching out further to expand social networks and seeking new romantic connections. The relationship with family is still the foundation, but adults experience much more dynamic connections.

Relationships do not just happen. A lot of work goes into making a relationship work. Interactions are dictated by different things which include the age of the people involved, the duration of time they have known each other, the context of their relationship among other factors. The way people behave and interact with other people is a direct result of experiences from the past. The most important thing to remember when it comes to relationships is to keep them healthy and functional. Young adults, more than any other demographic experience far more dynamic relationships and situations in which interactions occur. Our well-being is intrinsically tied to the quality of relationships in our lives.

Evaluating Social Relationships

These are the ones that are closest to an individual, comprising of the most intimate romantic relationships to the most formal professional connections.

Relationships end up falling apart due to neglect and poor communication. To keep them alive, we should be vigorous in attending to them to achieve the most out of them. Try taking time off of your busy schedule to connect with the people in your life. Appreciate their existence in your life and make them feel valuable. Get out of your head and be present whenever you are around them. Make sure you are listening to their concerns and understanding their point of view during discussions. Learn to communicate effectively about issues in the relationship with being confrontational and aggressive. Take responsibility for when you make a mistake and apologize while also forgiving mistakes of the other party.

When evaluating your relationships, look to see if the following signs are present. They are not always obvious, but it is important to spot these changes. Whenever being in this relationship is emotionally taxing because trying to predict the mood of your partner an takes a toll on your mentality, perhaps it is time to move on. A lot of passive aggressive behavior becomes present, taking many forms and killing the relationship slowly. Hostility ensues and makes one feel uncomfortable to even be around the other party. Sometimes moods keep changing and your end up having a perfect time with each other, and sometimes you hate also being around each other. This kind of volatility cannot sustain a relationship. When one party starts to make snide remarks toward the other that are disguised as jokes tends to cause an issue. This causes the victim to feel belittled and powerless on account of emotional bullying and is even made to seem like they are making a big deal out of nothing. It can feel like you are always walking on eggshells, afraid of setting off an argument over the most insignificant things. Trust should be the foundation of any relationship. Whenever that trust between people in a relationship is broken, they may find it difficult to feel secure about the way their partner interacts with other people. When a situation arises where it feels like they are a child and need to ask permission for them to do even the most basic things, perhaps it is time to end the relationship. This diminishes the victim's confidence in their life choices by getting used to checking in with their partner. This eventually leads to isolation from friends and family because of jealousy and insecurity.

Relationships define us and are part of the way we express ourselves. Positive relationships should bring out what is positive within us and improve and grow it. It is possible to change the dynamic of the relationship by figuring out what is going wrong and speaking to our partners. Once they have been made to understand that the relationship is on the verge of collapse and there is room for change and improvement, only then can the transformation begin.

If a solution can not be reached, it is time to shed that old skin and start fresh. Getting rid of these meaningful relationships can be hard, but completely manageable. It is only you that can control your life and you should be able to determine what makes you happy.

Start by officially ending the relationship. Express yourself clearly to your partner on the reasons why you feel the relationship must come to an end. Tell them that they were instrumental in gaining experiences that you will carry forward and learn from. This will bring you to the stage where you will need to get rid of the things you accumulated during the relationship. It will be hard due to sentiment, and you will want fond memories to stay with you, but you must remember that you are trying to move on. Next, determine what is important to you in life and other relationships. Make it a priority so you can start to feel better about yourself. Ending a relationship frees up time in your daily schedule. It is finally time to take care of yourself. Maybe pick a new hobby or learn a new skill. This way any negative thoughts that may arise from letting go will be pushed back. You will find keeping yourself busy will keep your positive mood alive. Reach out to the people you alienated while you were struggling in the toxic relationship. Receiving care and support from more positive relationships can be instrumental in the healing process. Don't be surprised if your partner reaches out; it has been known to happen. Set a boundary and limit the amount of contact you have with this person. Make sure they understand that it was for your good that you ended the relationship.

Moving on is hard, but if you take it a step at a time, you can find that you are well on your way to achieving the emotional stability you deserve. Don't be scared to put yourself out there. No two people are the same, and you have learned how to maintain positivity in the relationship. Feelings for the person you let go of sometimes linger. Do not rekindle the relationship. Remind yourself of the reasons why you ended the relationship.

Evaluating Social Media and its Effects on Relationships

The popularity of social media has been growing every day for the past ten years. Most of us have some form of social media profile, using them to connect with friends, distant relatives, conduct business and in some cases find romantic partners. Social media has made the world a much smaller place and people from all walks of life can interact with each other with the click of a button. So much good comes from social media, but on the used the wrong way, a lot of negativity can spread and ruin lives as well as relationships.

Social media affects relationships as well as in everyday life. Since a lot of people use social media to connect with their loved ones as well, it is impossible to rule out its effects on our interactions. It inspires jealousy among partners when one has to wonder who they significant other is interacting with privately. Unfaithfulness tends to occur mostly because there is no accountability, your social media account is yours, and you, therefore, feel autonomy and confidence you will not get caught. Lack of privacy occurs when one partner begins to share private information with their follower, thereby indirectly inviting strangers into the relationship. Suddenly people you don't know are influencing the relationship and causing further conflict.

Social media affects how we communicate. If both partners are always looking at their screens instead of getting to know one another, the relationship may be doomed from the start. Social media could be useful for long-distance relationships, giving the participants a platform on which to interact. However, a lot of how it is used today could not possibly help enhance a relationship. Be careful to minimize the use of social media when the relationship is still new. At this stage, it is vital that both partners get to know each other and learn how to make each other happy. It is also advisable to minimize jokes and sarcasm over text messages; they do not always have the same effect as they would if delivered in person. Keep your private life of the internet, not everyone who reads it has the best intention. Avoid posting personal opinions and conversations for everyone to see. Do not reply to a text message or post while being fueled by emotion. Take a moment to understand the message before responding. This will save you and your partner from an ugly misunderstanding. Make a clear distinction between your loved ones and other people you interact with on social media. Avoid doing the same thing for them that you would do for strangers. Make them feel special by putting extra effort into your interactions with them.

If the relationship is doomed and you have chosen to move on from it, there are social media related thing that must be done to purge the negativity of the old relationship. Go ahead and unfollow them from social media. Always having to look at them and being bombarded with information about them will set you back on your journey of healing. Control your emotions and avoid sharing the details of the breakup publicly. Find a trusted friend or family member vent to them. Exposing these intimate details on the internet may not have the intended effect and may cause you problems in the future. People you try to get close to may find your behavior off-putting. If your relationship was affected negatively by social media, do not repeat the same mistake. Have a more real-world relationship and be present. You could choose to cut social media off entirely or choose to keep only your relationship away from the public.

Evaluating the Effects of Social Media on Life

Social media has been found to have a surprisingly adverse impact on people. A lot of what is uploaded on these sites is manufactured to present people as something they are not. For someone who does not know any better, they may start to compare themselves and their lifestyles to those being portrayed online. People have ended up in debt over trying to lead a lifestyle they cannot afford. Negative body images are everyone on the internet. Only people who look a certain way are shown respect. The culture of celebrity worship is even more rampant. Hair, makeup and clothing trends are followed religiously. Non-conformists are seen outsiders and are bullied mercilessly to the point of self-hatred and in extreme cases, suicide. Some people overshare and are left open to identity theft, stalking, and fraud. The anonymity of the internet allows malicious people to operate and trap their victims easily.

Many signs can point to the need to cut back. Addicts start to substitute human connection with the relationships they make online. They experience anxiety when they cannot access the internet. They start to be withdrawn and psychologically absent even in social settings. They are always checking their phones even when they have not received any notifications. Eventually, they will stop going out in general and spend every waking moment on the internet. This behavior will ultimately lead to loneliness, low self-esteem, irritability, lack of productivity and depression.

Cutting back on social media is not easy, especially not for people who are addicted. Start small by limiting use to one device. Log off and delete the social media apps from every other device you own and leave only one option. Control access by setting up a usage schedule. Set aside periods when using social media is allowed. Avoid morning and bedtimes; these may hinder productivity. Take a break from social media for thirty days. Use this extra time to retrain your brain and keep your mind off of the withdrawal you are going through.

Pay attention to other areas of life you have been neglecting. Turn off notifications on your phone to help you resist the urge to check your phone and relapse. Respond to the milestones your loved ones make offline. Call or visit them to deliver gifts and messages. Set up rules for when you can access the internet. You can even use this as an incentive to be more productive. Reward yourself every time you accomplish something. Involve your friends to challenge you and do a fun bonding exercise for your relationship. Understand that social media does not add any actual value and that there is no reason to spend so much time connecting with strangers. Seek the help of a professional counselor or a therapist if going about this by yourself feels like too much of a burden. Get to the root of what caused you to turn to social media as a means to cope. It is an addiction like any other. Find ways to deal with your issues and recover.

Addiction to social media should not be confused with the use of social media. They need to exhibit the symptoms previously talked about if they are to be considered addicted. Most people enjoy being able to connect with people outside their physical boundaries.

Chapter 5: Changing Your Lifestyle

"You say, 'If I had a little more, I should be very satisfied.' You make a mistake. If you are not content with what you have, you would not be satisfied if it were doubled." - Charles Spurgeon. 1834.

Making a Change in Your Finances

Finance is the backbone of modern human society. We always need it, and we're always spending it. Quality of life is sometimes measured in the amount of wealth someone has. Having too much of it can be because people to become selfish and arrogant. Accumulating money can feel like a trap, sinking deeper with the more you have. Making the change from a lifestyle of excess can instantly change your life. If you are looking to save some money for a specific financial goal, deciding to become healthy is going to save you some much-needed cash. You don't have to change everything about your life. There are a few skills you need to have to cut back. Commitment to the goal, overcoming the fear of what is not familiar, dreaming big to motivate you to keep going and following through with the rules you set for yourself.

Exercise is a great way to start cutting back. That does not mean joining a fancy gym and adding to your expenditure. Don't pay for gym memberships when exercise can happen anywhere and can involve the most basic daily activities. Instead of spending fuel by driving to run errands, walk or run in order to burn calories. Engage in outdoor activities and games within your communities and get fit while simultaneously saving money.

Start to look into your daily routine and see what expensive and useless habits you have. If you spend money daily on junk food and soft beverages or smoking cigarettes, you can cut back, and you will realize you have money to spare. Minimize your social drinking or cut yourself off completely. Avoid sale offers as they trick you into believing that you are spending less, but in reality, you will be spending more in the long run.

Reduce the number of times that you go out to eat or order in. Introduce home cooking to your meal plan. Buying groceries and preparing your own meals is cheaper than paying for already prepared meals and transport costs. It also reduces calorie intake since a lot of people like to order fast food. Your meal budget may reduce by half if you start to prepare your own meals.

Switch to fresh foods. Processed food usually adds to the number of calories you take in, not to mention the excessive amounts of fat, salt, and sugar. There is a belief that going organic is actually more expensive than the alternative. The key thing here is the choice. Do not go for organic produce sold in stores or supermarkets. Visit the local markets and pick out what you like for a low price. Go for produce that is in season. This applies especially for fruits. Otherwise, you will end up paying a lot more for out of season produce.

If your place of work offers employee health benefits, take advantage of the opportunity to save on health insurance. This applies to retirement benefits as well. There are also ways of saving within the organization that is through financial programs, where employees are encouraged to save a little out of their income toward better health care and could double up as retirement funds after they retire.

Try as hard as you can to get out of debt. Debts always make it difficult to save money for important things. Most people enter adulthood with the weight of student loans already on their shoulders. After cutting out useless expenditure and putting away enough for a rainy day, start paying back people you owe and other debts you have accumulated over the years. You don't need to pay everything back immediately, but paying your debts needs to be a priority.

Avoid using credit cards instead of cash. It may be a safer option, but credit cards always tempt you to spend more than you need to and are followed up by hefty charges and interests. Debit cards are a better alternative or just carry cash. You only spend what you need to since you are spending the money you have.

Automate your finances, so that reduces the stress of thinking about finances. Start small with automating bill payments and deposits. Keep going until you have a mostly paperless system. This reduces the clutter you have lying around and is a more secure system of finance. You can check the transactions online, and you don't have to worry about losing receipts. Remember to keep checking your accounts to make sure everything is running smoothly.

Always have a budget whenever you go out shopping. If you want to grow your finances, don't ever spend more than you make. Budgets apply to everyone even people who make six figures. Don't allow yourself to fall into the pit of consumerism. Buy only what you need but only if it is within your budget.

Always remember that it is not mandatory to do all of these things at once. Take your time adopting a change so that you can get used to it. These changes are meant to be long term, and there really is no hurry.

You don't have to keep numerous bank accounts. Choose around four, if you need to have multiple accounts. Monitoring financial activity for many bank accounts can be complicated. Only have what you absolutely need and monitor it closely.

Do not allow money to run your life. Real pleasures and happiness cannot be bought. Prioritizing it as the single most important thing above all other relations is the wrong way to go about life. Take up a job that is fulfilling to you instead of the huge salary. Make it about passion instead of success. Budgeting and spending less will simplify your life, and you will find you will live a much simpler healthier life.

Minimalism Means Freedom

Living a simple life is not meant to drain all the fun from life. It simply means putting more value in things that matter. In figuring out what is important in life, we can experience freedom other people will look for but never find. Freedom to live stress-free, freedom to be more creative, freedom from distractions, freedom from negativity any other freedom you seek, you can achieve by becoming minimalist.

Opportunities to pursue passions and interests arise out of letting go of useless things that are taking up time in your life. Growth is inevitable when there is time to pay attention to what adds value and brings fulfillment. We can look deep within ourselves and figure out who we are and what we what.

Free time to spend with family members and other people we value allows relationships to improve and become stronger. We become more conscious and aware of what goes on around us. We are more likely to appreciate the world and life if we can truly see what goes on.

There is peace in the freedom created by living minimally. There are no longer ties that keep us trapped in one place or in a particular situation. We are free to do whatever we want in the pursuit of fulfillment. We can travel, explore, change and evolve into better people. Financial and psychological freedom allows us to survive on very little and improvises what we need—no more killing ourselves slowly working to earn a living at a place where we hate. It is about focusing on making ourselves and those around us happy. We give more while we take less.

Finding ourselves allows us to begin our journeys toward self- fulfillment. Everything we accomplish as minimalists is sure to bring us some form of benefit. We are aware of our motivations for doing things.

We are more in touch with the community. We spread positivity and inspire others to follow in our footsteps. We are doing the most we can for others, and we are rewarded by fulfillment. We take care of the earth because, in its own way, the earth takes care of us.

A lot of people believe that minimalism is boring. It is not. When people only see the surface of what minimalism is about, they are bound to form misconceptions about it. They only see the laid-back style, limited socializing and seemingly bland décor and draw false conclusions. Again, minimalism is not about what is there physically, but what we gain by downgrading to a simpler life. There are also different types of minimalism that different personalities would be comfortable enough to adopt.

Making the Change

Suddenly, you are feeling overwhelmed with the thoughts of altering your life. You are unfulfilled in the way you're living now. You want it to change. But you have no idea where to even start. You are beginning to feel overwhelmed with the choice and are contemplating turning back. Don't give up yet; follow the following step to change your life successfully.

Get insight into the stranger aspects of your life. Go deep into areas you never go and start to evaluate what is missing or in need of repair. Make notes of things that have veered your life off-course and set goals.

What was it that led you to make the decision to change your life? Usually, there are challenges that we just can't seem to overcome that make us start to evaluate ourselves. Be honest in making these evaluations as they are going to inspire what to change.

During this evaluation, you will come to the realization that some areas of your life are worse off than others. Your social life might be suffering while your professional life is thriving. You want to change your look and become healthier. Make these distinctions honestly since only you have control over your life.

Do you have an objective for making the change? Do you want to learn a new skill? Do you want to travel more? An objective helps you to figure out how you will change and drives you toward your goal.

Commitment is everything. You can have the most valid reasons for wanting change, but without commitment, you will not achieve anything. Going out of our comfort zones can be scary, but it is not impossible. Just remind yourself of the reward at the end.

Going through this process gives the perfect opportunity to learn more about yourself. You learn how much you can endure, what your purpose in life truly is, how determined you can be to make something happen. It also allows us to evaluate our beliefs. These can either push us forward or drive us back. We can encourage ourselves and root out beliefs that will derail our progress.

Remember, there will always be hurdles that may be difficult to overcome. Challenges are a part of everyday life. Don't give up at the first sign of struggle or be afraid to fail. Visualize the outcome you want and keep that image in mind. It will get you through the toughest times.

There are some things that you need to keep in mind while you go through the process of changing your life.

The attitude you have will make or break your efforts. The more positivity you exude, the more positive results you are likely to get.

Your emotional intelligence helps you to understand and manage your own emotions while also understanding those of others. This ability must be cultivated over time in order to reap benefits. Look at how intentionally you react to thoughts and choices and monitor how it affects your positivity.

Keep in mind that a lot of times reactions influence attitude. In an effort to change your life, you will have to change the way you react to situations as well. You cannot change what happens, but you can react to it in any manner and in doing so change the outcome completely.

Know when to let go. This is not the same as giving up. You don't always have to win. If pursuing something is draining your positivity, there is no point in fighting for it any longer.

Make sure to let it be known how you feel. Express your discontent, disappointment, frustrations, and anger to a trusted friend and this keeps things honest and eases a burden that has been weighing on your mind. This will help you maintain a positive outlook and be more motivated to change.

Be thankful for everything and everyone that you have. There is always someone who is worse off than you. Reinforcing positivity and gratitude will help you experience a more positive and fulfilling life.

So how do you make sure that you stick to the plan? Set realistic goals. Don't bite off more than you can chew. There is only so much you can handle. Enjoy yourself every step of the way. Don't take yourself too seriously and keep yourself jovial. Keep your friends and family close to support you. They should support your choices and challenge you to be better. Do not allow negative influences around you. If you can, seek out a life coach. It's always good to have a professional around.

A lot of the things we believe about ourselves and others have deterred the way we go through life. We compare progress and success to the progress and success of others. We start to think that we are not good enough for the things we want and therefore stop trying to achieve them. It is time to start changing your story. Think about yourself remove the mentality of "anyone else." Believe in your own worth and stick to that story. Use your emotions to support your new story. However, you will not be able to accomplish anything by just thinking about it. Go out and put in the effort. Challenge yourself and be assertive when it comes to what you want. Encourage yourself often and keep yourself positive.

Chapter 6: Mental Minimalism

"The secret of happiness, you see, is not found in seeking more, but in developing the capacity to enjoy less." - Socrates. 469 BCE.

Minimalism can't just be about reducing your stuff to fit in a suitcase. The principles applied for decluttering the house can also be utilized for the mental space. The mind is the central processing unit of our bodies and from time to time needs someone to look under the hood and remove what no longer works. Many people are focusing on everything else except mental health.

To practice a minimalist lifestyle, you need to have a change in your mindset. What your mind decides to work on is what you shall work on. A shift in one's way of thinking could be the sole reason minimalism works for someone and fail for someone else. The reason it may work faster for someone and take a long time for another. Because we are all different people, being mindful of ourselves is essential when trying out minimalism in our day to day lives.

Our minds are not built to deal with more than a couple of things at a time. We are great multitaskers, but there has to be a limit to what we take on in our minds. Otherwise, stress kicks in and is followed by a myriad of problems in the body. Decluttering the mind is just as important as decluttering your living space. Your mind is where your best ideas and ambitions live. They shouldn't have to share their home with silly things that don't serve any purpose in our lives.

It is true that one cannot eliminate worry and other things from the mind, but some practices enable one to deal with these negative thoughts. Cognitive errors that have clouded our minds for such a long time have to be addressed before we can live our best lives. People practicing minimalism realize that working on deep-rooted problems is the solution to many of the physical problems we have.

For example, some people place a lot of value in stuff because they didn't have them when they were young. The trauma of poverty makes them purchase things and refuse to let go for fear that they will be back to a time where they had nothing. While this may be a valid concern for someone, if they dig deep, they will realize that buying stuff instead of investing can lead to their greatest fear. Minimalism forces you to confront your deepest darkest fears in your subconscious.

Mental minimalism forces someone to focus on one thing at a time, that is, the present. Given that the past is already set in stone and no longer serves you, while the future is unknown and could very well be shaped by what happens now, it is safe to conclude that nothing matters more than dealing with now.

One should think of the mind a rental storage space. The more you add without removing stuff that no longer serves a purpose, the less space you will have for more important things. Unfortunately, there is no renting any other storage space; you have that small limited space for years. Learning how to declutter the mind could be the solution for stress and other mental illnesses.

When your mind is clear, you can now start focusing on your dreams and short-term goals. True minimalists know that other people may judge your choices, but they can't take away the results that minimalism can have in your life. Letting go of the need to impress people that don't care about things that are too expensive anyway can help you start focusing on what matters more to you. Nothing will bother you if you don't allow it to clutter your mind.

Minimalism helps someone address the consumerism mentality. This refers to that scarcity mentality that kicks in when you see a sale or a new advertisement from your favourite brand. Minimalists don't spend most of their time thinking of different ways to spend money because the fundamental principle of minimalism is that less is more. The problem with consumerism is that it encourages people to spend their money and when that is gone, they should borrow and keep spending. When you realize that, you will be in a better position to discern needs from wants. The trick here is to cut out excess spending instead of going cold turkey slowly. The mind doesn't adjust when abrupt changes are made as they will reject the new ideas. The mind also needs to learn slowly and see small changes so that it becomes more receptive. That is how it forms new habits, by repeating the same concept for an extended period.

Could Minimalism be the Answer to Anxiety and depression?

Our minds can be complicated even for us. Many things can lead to anxiety and depression that may be out of our control but suppose there was something we could do to stop them from creeping in.

One thing that we can be sure about is that anxiety and depression can lead to clutter in our homes and relationships. If we can't deal with what is going on in the mind the ripple effect can certainly be felt in other areas of our lives. People with depression tend to sleep a lot and do nothing the whole day, not because they are lazy but because they are dealing with a lot in their minds. That leaves no room for cleaning or even maintaining a healthy relationship with close family and friends.

What does mental clutter do to the mind that inevitably leads to anxiety and depression?

It tends to shift our attention away from what we are supposed to do and focuses it to what is not as important. For example, instead of one focusing on their studies, they end up thinking of problems at home that they can do nothing about.

It makes on fidgety and unable to calm down and relax. When the mind is scattered so is the body. It can lead to insomnia or hallucinations in extreme cases.

It makes the mind focus on what has not yet been done. The mind would then dwell on the failed tasks rather than the successful tasks already completed.

It causes feelings of overwhelming when decluttering anything comes to mind. It doesn't allow the mind to tackle small tasks. Instead, it makes everything look hard and undoable. This causes anxiety, and eventually, nothing gets done.

It would be unfair if I didn't say that minimalism is not a cure for anxiety and depression. What it does is give you a different way of viewing things and life in general. It allows you to lighten the mental load that is keeping you from doing anything. The gratification that comes with accomplishing small tasks can lead to one feeling happier and happier. It should by no means be a substitute for getting help and addressing the underlying causes of these mental problems.

Minimalism forces people to address who they are and leads one on a journey of self-discovery. It forces you out of your mind and enjoys everything that you have instead of wishing you have more. T separates you from limiting beliefs such as you need material things to be happy. You soon realize that you are still you even if you have less stuff or nothing at all. You end up achieving your purpose in life and start working towards making it a reality. Your priorities change tremendously, and it is safe to say they you mature a little more because of shedding your old self.

It can, however, tackle mild anxiety and depressions caused by mental clutter. When you start feeling that you are not operating at 100%, you might want to look at what is going on in your mind.

Positive Impacts of Minimalism on Mental Health

Minimalism coupled with professional help can be a great way to keep your mental health at an all-time high. As I keep repeating, minimalism is about changing the core of who you are to be who you want to be. If you feel like you have tried everything and nothing seems to be working, minimalism can be the answer you have been seeking. It may take time before one sees results, but the challenge of living a clutter-free life can keep your mind occupied enough to keep negative thoughts at bay.

1. Minimalism and finance

Many people lose a lot of money through overspending and impulse buying. Minimalism encourages you to look at what you are spending your money on and evaluate if it adds value or not. More often than not, many people end up saving a ton of money when they cut out unnecessary spending. Financial insecurity has caused a lot of people anxiety and depression especially those that have families that depend on them. Minimalism encourages people to use the money they save wisely and on things that are important. One can even take that vacation they had been postponing because they had no extra money to spend which can boost their morale even further.

2. Minimalism and Confidence

Nobody wants their family and friends visiting when their house is a mess because of shame and guilt. This causes a strain in your relationships as people will begin to wonder about your living situation. Loneliness can be associated with anxiety and depression as someone has no one to tell them that their negative thoughts are false. Decluttering the home and the mind gives you a boost of confidence that you need because you will no longer be afraid to let people into your space.

3. Minimalism and Energy

Depression and anxiety are characterized by low energy to perform the required tasks. This is a problem because a person lives by going something every day. A person's purpose is what drives them every morning to wake up and do something constructive. Minimalism can help someone make healthy food choices that boost their energy.

4. Minimalism and Individuality

Although minimalism is a trend that many people have adopted today, it is a personal and individual journey to undertake. A person suffering from anxiety or depression caused by feelings of inadequacies or comparisons on social media or life, in general, can benefit immensely from this practice. Taking over a challenge that encourages you to deal with your most in-depth issues can be an excellent way to learn more about yourself and do everything to improve.

5. Minimalism and Decision Making

Minimalism involves making choices, both big and small every day. A person that is plagued with indecisiveness will have to overcome this fear because they will be forced to make choices every day. Starting from small decisions like which pair of jeans to keep or donate to more substantial decisions like letting go of toxic relationships. After some time, making decisions will be a regular thing because you will be able to understand the impact it shall have in your life.

6.   Minimalism and Time

Time may be a limited resource and anxiety, and depression takes up a lot of it by keeping a person prisoner. By working on what makes themselves, people with these issues will understand how to value their time and do something constructive with it. It also helps people respect the process, making them more conscious about the time it takes to be true minimalists. They are also able to share their time with others through volunteering or something as simple as spending time with family and friends.

Emotional Minimalism

We as humans have something that separated us from all other beings in the world, emotions. We have many positive and negative feelings that we go through every day depending on the situations we are in. They are why we do things; they are how we react to situations; they are who we are sometimes. Emotions are inevitable as long as we have breath and what we need to understand is that we can't let them rule our lives.

A person that is governed by his or her emotions faces a lot of challenges in life. If you are always angry, no one will want to be around you. If you are too nice, people will take advantage of you. The need to balance out your emotions to live a healthy life can be quite challenging, and most of us fail every day. That doesn't mean that we shouldn't try to do better.

Our ability to carry emotional clutter is unrivaled which is sad. Many people are actually in denial concerning the internal turmoil that is going on within them. Some people keep within themselves repressed and unacknowledged emotions that are sometimes referred to as emotional baggage. Many of us don't want to deal with feelings as they occur and prefer to push it down or put it off completely. Unfortunately, feelings have to come out somehow and the more they are bottled up, the worse it shall be when they eventually do surface. Emotions like grief and rejection usually act faster and make us sick from inside. The best minimalist way to avoid this is to confront instead of dodging. Deal with emotions as they arise because they won't affect you in the long run. It will hurt for a while, but eventually, all will be well.

Holding back emotions of betrayal, hatred, and bitterness can also make you sick from within. The person you hate so much may not experience the same feelings as you, and that can even make your grudge worse. A minimalist would take their time to evaluate why this person's actions have caused him or her such pain. More often than not, the answer usually lies with you. It is said that anger toward a person is like shooting yourself and expecting the other person to die. If we work on our understanding of others and cultivating forgiveness when wronged, we do not give such emotions power over us

Too much expectation causes us to feel bad when other people fail to meet our standards. As parents, as romantic partners, we all project our unfair expectations on others and don't allow them room to fall short. Most of the time we expect things and don't necessarily communicate what we think the other person should do. We should accept that other people are different and will not always feel the same way we do. Minimalism enables us to recognize that people are imperfect and they are working on themselves the same way we are.

Cognitive errors in the mind allow us to speak negativity to ourselves. Feelings of inadequacy come from a long time of hearing bad things about ourselves. It may be hard to pinpoint precisely when some of these negative thoughts started, but we can choose to nip them in the bud. It is not easy to just let go of the feelings you have had for years but acknowledging them is the first step to change.

There are also some negative emotions that come when one decides to start a minimalist lifestyle. One feels overwhelmed when they look at the amount do work that comes with this lifestyle. There is also recycler's remorse that occurs when one needs to get rid of their material possessions. All these are emotions brought by fear of change and do not hold any ground when one analyses them.

Chapter 7: Maintaining the Lifestyle

"One of the advantages of being born in an affluent society is that if one has any intelligence at all, one will realize that having more and more won't solve the problem, and happiness does not lie in possessions, or even relationships: The answer lies within ourselves. If we can't find peace and happiness there, it's not going to come from the outside - Tenzin Palmo. 1943.

As with anything else in life, the first step is hard but the subsequent steps are harder. Making a habit out of action can seem like a hard task to achieve, but once you make a conscious decision to live a minimalist lifestyle, you can get over any hurdles that you are faced with.

The most important question to ask is WHY. For example, A person may choose to be a minimalist because they have seen that they have been affected by consumerism. He or she, therefore, chooses to live minimally so that he or she can save some money and enjoy the things he or she already has. Changing what you know for the unknown can be hard and soon, it may be a challenge to keep up with the habit. But a person may check their finances and see that they have more money in the bank than they did initially because they no longer overspend or shop on impulse. This can be a motivating factor for the minimalist that encourages them to keep on keeping on.

How then can a minimalist maintain the minimalist lifestyle permanently?

1. Keep the things that you need and frequently use in your home

Despite the constant pressures from today's society to own the biggest, the flashiest and the trendiest, you will learn that you don't need any of that to be happy. If something serves you well and is in good condition, there is no need to upgrade to a new version of it. Nit-pick everything that you allow into your home.

2. Keep your home clutter free

A minimalist understands the importance of decluttering and should make a habit out of it, even when he or she doesn't feel up to it. This is because they understand how things can pile on and eventually one gets overwhelmed and learns to live with the mess. Whenever stuff starts to pile up, deal with the mess immediately. If it is laundry, dishes, mail, etc., set a routine for yourself that allows you to work on them weekly. When you purchase something, get rid of the empty container or the old thing. There is no point in keeping two items that serve the same purpose. A routine becomes a guide for a minimalist lifestyle.

3. Change your mindset

For any minimalist to have lived a successful minimal lifestyle, they must change the way they see things. It is easy for you to maintain your lifestyle if you understand its importance in your life. For most successful minimalists, they wouldn't want to go back to their lives before. They don't feel like they deny themselves a good life, but instead, they feel like they are making more room for what matters most to them.

4. Find other minimalists

Many people find fellow minimalists to motivate each other in a community of people with the same interest. You will learn how other minimalists maintain their lifestyle, and you can share your challenge with people that understand your struggle. There are books, blogs, groups on social media that share other people minimalism journeys that you can relate to. Look for a community that will inspire you to keep up the habit.

5. Don't keep storage bins

If you have somewhere to store your junk, you will keep it. This happens for people with a lot of storage spaces such as attics, basements, and garages where they don't see the mess. After decluttering, everything that isn't being used every day should be evaluated and all extra storage bins should be removed from the house. The only storage bins that should remain are those that hold seasonal items like Halloween and Christmas decorations, seasonal clothes or camping equipment.

Overcoming Purging Remorse

It is very common for a person that wants to get rid of their things to wonder if they might need it later. When one thinks like that, they immediately start looking for excuses to keep the item. The same goes for friendships and intimate relationships. One may want to focus on the right time they shared and forget how toxic their lives have become since allowing this person in their life. It is hard to let go of anything that someone has had for a long time hence the mess they have accumulated in their life. You might want to run the item, habit or person through a series of questions that might help you gain some clarity.

- What is the worst thing that can happen if I decide to let go? This question enacts all possible scenarios that might result from cutting out something from your life. Is it worth it finally? More often than not, it turns out that all the negative thoughts are in your head.

- How would I deal with this choice if I wasn't afraid of the consequences? This question allows you to remove fear from the equation for a moment to pick a solution without prejudice. Sometimes the fear of loss is what keeps us entangled in messes and toxicity and without it, we would be better off.

- If anything were to happen now, would it still matter as it does now? This question helps you determine if something is still as valuable as it once was. If your house were to burn down, is it something that you would spend money to repurchase? If I moved away, would I still be friends with this person?

All these stages help you overcome the sense of regret that you might have if you let go of what you know or have. But what can one do move past the remorse of letting go of things and people that no longer serve a purpose in one's life? The answer might be simple, but it does require some soul searching. Keep the things that hold meaning in your life and let go of what doesn't. If you are still anxious about the choice to make, it might be something that ties the item or relationship to your subconscious. You will then have to seek professional help to help you unpack the emotional baggage related to whatever you cannot let go of.

Learning New Skills that Promote Minimalism as a Habit

There is a name for the habit of finding new ideas and keeping them stashed away without actually implementing them. It is called the 'Shiny Object Syndrome'. Minimalist can end up as a stashed away idea if one doesn't have the will to practice it every day of their life. We all understand that life sometimes becomes challenging and some things are just not as crucial anymore. Minimalism should be viewed as a way of life and not only as a passing trend if one is to practice it successfully. Learning new skills need not be a chore that minimalists feel they have to learn. It should be fun and a way to keep the first fire burning in them.

When you spend enough time scouring the internet, you shall see that most people search for learning skills that make them happy, feel less alone, survive or improve how they relate with others. People will always gravitate towards being good at something that they have always wanted to do despite not learning it in school. There are many skills for a minimalist to learn to maintain the minimalism lifestyle whether it is relevant or not. They end up learning a skill that brings them joy in the end and not just to be a better minimalist. Some skills that enable one to be a better minimalist are:

1. Recycling

A minimalist at the core learns the importance of their environment and how to keep it clean. They can teach themselves how to keep their surroundings as natural as they possibly could. Learning how to recycle plastics is just one example of recycling. Reusing old containers for other purposes other than what they were intended for is also a healthy minimalist practice.

2. Donation

Many people need things that are causing a mess in your home. You do not need fifty pairs of shoes because you can never wear them all. If something no longer fits or spark joy, take it to the homeless shelters, donation boxes or church depending on your location. Some people keep a donate box close by so that they can fill it up with things that they would wish to give. The donate box can be taken to donation centers once a month if it fills up quickly or twice annually if it doesn't.

3. Volunteering

People in need don't just need material things; they need people to show love, care, and concern about their wellbeing. Spending your free time helping the elderly, reading to orphans or serving food for the homeless can be a good way to remember that you are incredibly fortunate to have some things. It's amazing how insignificant our problems are compared to others when we take the time to mingle with others.

4. Cooking

A way to save money or focus on fitness can be learning how to make your meals. Eating out may be extravagant and unhealthy for some people, and the only way they can work on it is by cooking at home. There is no need to take expensive cooking classes; there are plenty of YouTube channels that teach beginners how to cook healthy and tasty meals at home with simple ingredients.

5. Making lists and budgets

Learning how to plan your time and money is a good way for a minimalist to keep up with the lifestyle. Lists enable someone to keep track of what they have to do in a day, what they need to buy among others. Some of the most successful people in the world admit to writing down what they plan to do the following day in to-do lists. Tracking your spending through budgets can be an excellent way to keep yourself accountable for your financial goals. It can also be a good motivation when you find you have more money to spend at the end month because you cut out unnecessary spending.

It is Okay to Fail

One thing that minimalists need to understand is that this is not an exact science. There is no way for you to know if this is for you unless you try. One has to take the journey a day at a time until minimalism becomes a part of who they are. That being said, it is okay to struggle. It is also okay to fail. The thing that makes it worthwhile is if one tries, again and again, to keep the practice going. Staying motivated to maintain the lifestyle is hard for both beginners and veteran minimalists and anyone can have good and bad days.

You need to remember that minimalism is not a prison sentence that you cannot opt out of. If it isn't for you, there is no need to maintain the charade as you shall be unhappy if you do. If it is the lifestyle that you feel is for you, lower your expectation and take it one step at a time. It doesn't happen overnight, and it is not just about decluttering your home. Minimalism is a holistic experience that encourages people to look at all aspects of their lives and let go of what is no longer serving them.

You shall fail if you think of minimalism as a way of denying yourself things or just removing things. We know that nature abhors a vacuum. If you are only removing, cutting off, cleaning out, making room, then you shall be unhappy and end up not getting anything from this experience. You must remember that once you make room, space has to be filled with something positive.

Say one decided to quit smoking and drinking, as a minimalist practice dictated, one should use that money and time to make some positive change. One can volunteer and donate the money to a charity they believe in instead. Minimalism encourages people to change all aspects of their life, not just what people can see. It is a private journey for each minimalist as their whys are often very different.

For a minimalist to avoid failing, they need to think long and hard about what values they believe in and what is important to them. It is a hard question to answer if you are trying to unlearn a lot of things about yourself. Remember there is no wrong or right way to answer this question. The answers differ from person to person, but whatever one chooses, it should be their driving force.

People fail because they lose sight of why they started this exercise in the first place. They may even have started it for the wrong reason. If you decide to follow the way your minimalist friend is living without going through the soul searching first, you are doomed to fail. You are looking at your values and the only true way to see minimalism in a positive light rather than sacrificing comfort.

Minimalism is a slow process and shouldn't be rushed. Don't toss away things that you might need in future because you were in a hurry to declutter. Impulsive decisions can make someone abandon the minimalist lifestyle faster because they will be frustrated before they can enjoy anything. Minimalism should be viewed as a way of making do with just enough rather than getting rid of things.

It is important to note that there can be extreme minimalist that advocate for getting rid of everything that you are not using including, family trinkets, university diplomas among others. As I said, following other people journeys as if it is your own can lead to unhappiness and failure. The beauty of minimalism is that it can be customized to suit an individual. It should be treated as a pilgrimage of some sought that enables one to discover themselves and what they hold dear to them. Keep what works and ignore what doesn't for you. Don't be the minimalist that still keeps up with the Joneses.

Chapter 8: Lessons to Learn from Minimalism

"My riches consist, not in the extent of my possessions, but in the fewness of my wants." - Joseph Brotherton. 1783.

One of the lessons that a minimalist will eventually realize as time goes by is that nothing of what they get rid of now will matter tomorrow. It is what they feel after all the stuff they no longer need is gone than matters.

They will learn that memories are not attached to material possession but the mind.

A minimalist learns the hard way that all things will get better with time. The feeling of anxiety, regret, guilt among others shall linger for a while before they dissipate and one feels better.

One learns how to see the adverse effects of consumerism. You will become more conscious of the things that you buy. You will feel suffocated in a cluttered space and freer and more creative in a clear space.

You will learn to appreciate everything you have more. You will not waste time, money and effort on things that don't bring you joy.

Debunking Myths about Minimalism

The reason many people are skeptical about being minimalists is that of the fear they get when they hear some of the crazy myths that are circulating. Some myths also give people false hope that minimalism is easy and doesn't require one to do a lot to achieve success. Minimalism is just like riding a bike. You see someone riding, and you convince yourself that you can do it. But when you get on the bike, you struggle to keep the balance and eventually fall off. Just like riding a bike, only the people who approach minimalism like a life-changing experience will make it. You will fail, you will struggle, but you won't give up halfway before reaching your goals.

Myth 1: It is easy

If it were easy, then everyone would be doing it

Myth 2: One will see results overnight or after a long time

Minimalism isn't just about decluttering and tidying up. One has to change holistically to see any physical manifestation. It may be a short time for some and a long time for others depending on issues they have to address.

Myth 3: One loses their personality

On the contrary, one would be able to tell a minimalist's personality because it is no longer buried under heaps of clutter. You can tell his or her character from the way he or she dresses, his or her home décor, his or her relationships or his or her relationship with money.

Myth 4: It is boring

Nothing is boring about minimalism. Different assignments ensure a minimalist grows into who they want to be. It may take years before a person successfully masters minimalism. Some people think that minimalist wears the same clothes every day or wear only black outfits. That's just ignorant.

Myth 5: It removes from a house what makes it a home

Just because one removes what no longer serves them from a house doesn't mean that the memories are no longer there. People even say that home is where the heart is which is the case with minimalism. Just because you have less doesn't mean you have nothing.

Myth 6: It is hard to maintain

Yes and no depending on the reason you chose to be a minimalist. If you genuinely want to better yourself, then it is not hard to maintain, but if you are following your buddy, you might fail.

Myth 7: You are a nomad

Nomads are individuals who move and live in different places without setting their roots there. Just because your life can fit in a suitcase doesn't mean you can't settle in one place.

Myth 8: You are poor

Nothing about minimalism says that only poor people can practice. If anything, it advocates on few excellent quality items rather than many cheap ones. It also doesn't mean that minimalist count what they have. They own what they want in their lives and nothing more. Minimalists are also not freeloaders that have nothing and sleep on friends' couches.

Myth 9: You are self-centered

Despite being a practice that focuses on one's space and growth, minimalism also encourages people to look at and evaluate their close relationships. Some relationships have been saved thanks to practices learned from minimalism. Not all minimalists are single. It is for anyone that needs it.

Myth 10: It cannot be sustained in the long run

Minimalism is different for everyone. For some it works, for some, it doesn't. It is hard to tell for whom it will and for whom it, therefore, it is an individual journey. If one chooses to undertake the minimalism path and stick to it, you will find a way to sustain it for yourself by whatever means necessary.

Things You'll Wish You Knew Before Becoming a Minimalist

With the minimalism trend being adopted by more and more people, they need to realize that being a minimalist isn't just by name. You can't just add the word minimalist after your name and expect it to mean something. There is no prestige in being called a minimalist. It is a hard truth, but it is still the truth. Minimalism is more of the journey and not the destination. There is no easy way to be a minimalist, you are. No matter how hard you try, nothing will make your space look picture perfect. You will feel better because you let go of things that are holding you back, but it will not look pin-able on Pinterest.

Some people need to tidy up, not become minimalists. If your space is fine and needs some organization, then that's all you need to do. A minimalist is overwhelmed by things that they have and need to get rid of some things to feel better. Purging stuff from your space will be a continuous process as you change and grow in your journey.

As a minimalist, it is better to prepare yourself for setbacks in the future. You may do so well at the beginning, but sometimes things may not go as planned. Do not dwell so much on the setback because you may abandon the practice altogether. Take notes and purpose to do better in the future. A minimalist practice is to know where everything 'lives' so that when things are out of order, you can rearrange easily.

Not everyone will understand the lifestyle you have chosen. They will have opinions that may attempt to discourage you or ridicule you. But you must stay strong because you are the only one that needs to understand the process. People are always suspicious of things they do not understand. You may choose to engage them if you are close, but most of the time you can ignore what they are saying about you. Be prepared to hear that you have changed and might even be lucky enough to get an intervention!

Minimalism is a journey with discoveries every day. No one can say they have truly mastered the art. You may have family and friends, but you will need people who understand what you are doing. You will need likeminded individuals with a similar mindset to yours. They will help you vent when you are going through a rough time, and they will help you understand different practices. As we have learned before, it a never-ending learning process.

Even if you have to talk to like-minded people, you are on the journey alone. You will want to try out what someone else is doing that seems to be working. It may work for you or it may not. It is okay regardless of the outcome. There is no timeline; there is no plan. Minimalism is different for everyone, and the results are entirely different. It may be easy for someone else and hard for you. Don't start the process with unrealistic expectations.

You might want to buy things that look a little more minimalist than your stuff. Big mistake to be a minimalist you have to get rid of stuff, not adding it. Minimalism should not just be about what you have or don't have. The more you have, the more you need to ask yourself why. You might be tempted to purge until you have nothing, which is also not the ideal scenario. Minimalism is about a balance between having things and using everything you have.

Struggles of Being a Minimalist

Because of the recent trend of everyone suddenly embracing minimalism, one may assume that it is easy because everyone is doing it. It is not as simple as that because even people who have been practicing minimalism for an extended period still struggle.

1. How and where to start

Starting anything in life is never easy. Many people stick to that place where they say they want to do something and they never do. The same applies to minimalism especially when they realize that they may have to make some tough decisions. Some people lead hectic lives and feel like minimalism would take up a lot of their time and therefore never come around to it

2. Lack of support from family members and friends

Just because you have decided to simplify your way of life doesn't mean that your partner, parents or even friends will understand your decision. Some of them will try to talk you out of it, some will not be supportive, and others will just cut you out of their lives completely. Minimalism as a way of life can be confusing to people who don't understand it, and it can be especially harder if the people closest to you are skeptical about it. These are the same people that pressure you to buy more stuff to be on trend and fit in. They are usually the reason most people quit the experience in the early stages.

3. Guilt and regret

We have already talked about the remorse one feels when getting rid of things, they have worked so hard for. It is harder for hoarders to let go of stuff because they have tied their emotions to it. Learning to detach emotions from material possession is a practice that minimalists learn. They need to understand that even after getting rid of an item, the memories remain. Some people have to deal with their emotional baggage so that they can let go of the material possession which may require a professional. Some people keep things because they feel like it won't make economic sense to replace an item later.

4. Not falling prey to consumerism

Today's society has put a lot of importance in buying and owning a lot of things. You can't go two steps nowadays without an advertisement popping up. Impulse buying and shopping as a form of therapy are common ways people cope with stress and emotional distress. Learning how to control yourself around items can be a struggle for a minimalism novice. Many people use sales as an excuse to buy more and more things that they do not need.

5. Teaching children about minimalism

Parents have a hard time understanding the concept of minimalism themselves hence the dilemma when it comes time to prepare their young ones on its importance. We as adults already have a problem with detaching ourselves from material things. Imagine how children would feel if they have to let go of their favorite toys or books. It may be harder to convince a child to let go of their beloved items at first, but they learn by example.

Overcoming Minimalist Struggles

If you have started the journey, congratulations because you are halfway done. Even if you are struggling, remember that there are plenty of people that desire to start but do not know where to start from. Trying to peel back the layers of why you are so attached to material things and consumerism, in general, is a big deal in itself. Consider every day that you maintain the lifestyle to be a step closer to achieving freedom from all that was holding you back before.

For those that are struggling to take on the minimalism challenge, it will be hard, but it is worth it. Confronting hidden truths can be hard especially for people that are surrounded by skeptics. Trying something new alone can be daunting, but it can change our lives. Minimalism can transform your life and mindset if you allow yourself some discomfort at the beginning.

There comes a time that someone must accept that they need change. If everything else is not working, something new may be on the horizon if you are keen enough to look. Some people don't try something new because they worry about what others will say. It feels right to you, go for it. A life well lived cannot be lived for others. One has to look within, write down why minimalism is the path for them and trust the process.

Success stories always attract people. There are plenty of people who no one believed could make it based on the path they had chosen. When they succeeded, everyone wanted to know how they did it so that they could emulate. How ironic, right? The same applies to minimalism. You can follow the path less travelled and be an example to the people around you. They may not understand at first, but when they see how different your life is, they will come around.

It is part of the process to worry if the decision to declutter your life is the right one. You may even make excuses as to why you still need to hold on. That is normal for many people, but it is necessary to avoid the temptation to keep stuff you don't need. You shall be sad, guilty and even regret the decision but only for a short period. Working on the reasons you connect your emotions to material things can make the process easier.

By having less stuff, one learns to appreciate what they have more. If you have ten pens, you will not care if one gets lost. But if you had one that you like, you will take care of it because you know it's all you have. The same concept applies to relationships. Having less doesn't have to be boring. Consider interesting ideas like meal planning and capsule wardrobes that encourage you to try new things.

Minimalism forces someone to look deep within and find the root cause of everything that they do. Starting new habits without really looking into the root of the old ones can be a waste of time. It can help you uproot what no longer serves you from the source so that the bad practices can no longer sprout back.

Conclusion

There are plenty of success stories on the internet of minimalists that have been practicing for years. That is what we are all aiming to be. There may be people that regret starting the journey and some may have even given up along the way. As we have already discussed minimalism is an individual journey. Some may even begin to question the concept of less is more. It is okay for you as a beginner to look at all kinds of information so that when you choose to be a minimalist, you are all in and are not instructed by the noise.

The good thing about minimalism is that it offers a holistic change of the mind and physical. Even if one day you may decide to quit being a minimalist, the principles you learn will not be forgotten. Therefore, do this challenging thing selfishly. Make this something that transforms your life from mediocre to great.

Accept that there are some principles that you don't resonate with. For example, if a person doesn't care about going green, it doesn't mean that they do not care about the environment. As a minimalist, you will learn other ways that suit you and still take care of the environment. There is no need to feel guilty, and no one should make you feel like you have failed if some aspects are not for you.

As a minimalist, you will realize that all the principles that you have learned will trickle down to many other areas of your life. Your career and fitness journey may also benefit from minimalism as your outlook on things changes. A real minimalist embraces change because it is constant in minimalism. Minimalism allows an individual to take more risks in their career and life in general.

Many people are quitting their jobs to become globetrotters. These people may not necessarily be single people that have no obligations. Some families live on the road and are thriving because they have figured out a better way to go through life.

A real minimalist trains his mind to want less rather than just removing material possessions from his life. With a shift in mindset, the possibilities are endless. Since you are a beginner, you might be tempted to focus on the negative aspects of minimalism. To achieve great success, you must allow yourself to go through the process without external interference.

Bonus Material: Earning – An Introduction To Earning With The Double Your Income Sequence

SECTION 1: THE SECRET OF FORMING MONEY HABITS (AND HOW TO ENFORCE THEM)

You are a collection of your favorite habits.

And, you have a niche set of habits that contribute to the money you can earn and keep, during your average month. Understanding the science behind these habits will help you positively influence the energy you spend on making more money.

A habit is a practice that you have used so often, that it has become an internalized, autonomic blueprint – a kind of default program for how to execute a specific action.[1]

Habits become damaging when they stop being beneficial, and instead, become uncontrollable, unintentional and contrary to your personal goals. Most individuals carry with them the burden of many bad habits, which inadvertently keeps them from forging ahead and achieving their income goals.

According to Charles Duhigg, the reason why we struggle with habits is that they are as unique as we are. There is no quick-fix formula.

In order to effectively change your habits, you need enlightenment on a better process, and, on your stuck behavior. Then you can change your *cue-routine-reward* cycle.[2]

---

[1] Habit, Wikipedia, https://en.wikipedia.org/wiki/Habit
[2] Duhigg, Charles, How Habits Work, https://charlesduhigg.com/how-habits-work/

Cue: a trigger that puts your brain in automatic mode and chooses your habit

Routine: A physical, mental or emotional set of actions

Reward: What you gain from executing the habit

With fresh ideas and an understanding of how to break bad habit loops, you will adopt powerful new habits that will help you double your income every, single, month.

SECTION 2: HOW TO CREATE NEW MONEY HABITS

New habits are how you will double your income.

This means you need to:

#1: Identify and break bad habits, to free up room for fresh practices

#2: Identity and consciously adopt new habits, until they become automatic

This guide is not about the first step. If you want to learn how to break bad habits, I suggest reading Charles Duhigg's classic, "The Power of Habit."

What you do need to realize, is that a number of your existing habits need to change, to make room for the ones outlined in this guide. You must become consciously aware of your *cue-routine-reward cycle*, and interrupt it to stay on track.

You can do this effectively by replacing your existing rewards, with your new goal to double your income. To create a new habit, follow this simple process.

- **Identify the bad habit that must be replaced**
  - ➢ Waking up at 7 am to be at work at 8 am

- **Identify the harm it's causing**
  - ➤ Rushing and feeling harassed and irritated when you get to work
- **Understand and replace the reward from your bad habit**
  - ➤ Instead of instant gratification from sleeping late, your mood will be elevated, and your energy levels will be high at work
- **Implement the new habit, motivated by a stronger overall reward**
  - ➤ Practice waking up at 5 am, arriving at work at 7:30 and easing into your day, to stimulate the positive mindset required for success

According to modern studies, it takes roughly 66 days before a new behavior becomes automatic.3

---

[3] Lally, Phillippa, How are Habits Formed: Modelling Habit Formation in the Real World, https://onlinelibrary.wiley.com/doi/abs/10.1002/ejsp.674

SECTION 3: THE 14 HABITS THAT WILL DOUBLE YOUR INCOME

Here are the habits you need.

Habit 1: SLEEP (You're Not Doing It Right)

Bill Gates, the co-founder of Microsoft, sleeps for 7 hours every night and reads for 1 hour before bedtime.

With over a third of Americans not getting enough regular sleep, most people vastly underestimate the importance of quality shuteye in their lives.

Over or under-sleeping exposes you to increased risk for chronic conditions, mental distress, stroke and heart disease.[4] According to a 2018 Poll by The National Sleep Foundation, excellent sleepers feel more effective at getting things done the next day.[5]

The first habit you need to adopt is simple – get high quality, regular sleep.

Set a time every evening to go to sleep and stick to it. You should be in bed an hour before, your phone off and all screens far away from you. Read for an hour. Then, go to sleep for 7.

Wake up promptly, 7 hours later. Not a minute more.

Sticking to this new habit promises you stronger immunity, the improved concentration at work and greater emotional stability overall. Consistency will

---

[4] 1 in 3 Adults Don't Get Enough Sleep, https://www.cdc.gov/media/releases/2016/p0215-enough-sleep.html

[5] National Sleep Foundation's 2018 Sleep in America Poll Shows Americans Failing to Prioritize Sleep, https://sleepfoundation.org/media-center/press-release/2018-sleep-in-america-poll-shows

ensure that your circadian rhythms function well, and you never have trouble with restless sleep or with falling asleep.[6]

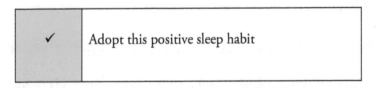

✓	Adopt this positive sleep habit

Habit 2: EXERCISE (It's Not Enough, or It's Too Much)

Ex-President Barack Obama works out for 45 minutes a day, six days a week. Thirty minutes or more of aerobic exercise is done daily by 76% of all successful people.7

Aerobic exercise is the one consistent habit that will give you the energy you need to succeed. You should run, walk, jog, bike or take a class at the gym. Cardio gets your blood pumping, which is ideal for your brain and boosts your intelligence.[8]

The second habit you need to adopt – find and practice an aerobic exercise, daily.

Now, you need to pick 45 minutes to an hour, every day to get your cardio in. It makes no difference whether you do this in the morning, or late in the evening – as long as it is done every single day.

Consistency is how you will reap these many benefits.

---

[6] Mahabir, Nicole, How and Why Waking Up at the Same Time Every Day Can Improve Your Health, https://www.cbc.ca/life/wellness/how-and-why-waking-up-at-the-same-time-everyday-can-improve-your-health-1.4357391

[7] Cohen Jennifer, Exercise is One Thing Most Successful People Do Everyday, https://www.entrepreneur.com/article/276760

[8] Regular Exercise Releases Brain Chemicals Key for Memory, Concentration, and Mental Sharpness, From the May 2013 Harvard Men's Health Watch, https://www.health.harvard.edu/press_releases/regular-exercise-releases-brain-chemicals-key-for-memory-concentration-and-mental-sharpness

Try to pick something that fits into your life, schedule and likes. You don't have to spend money, you simply have to get active. This means finding an exercise you will enjoy. Some people like boxing classes, others prefer to take a walk around the neighborhood.

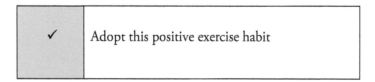

✓ Adopt this positive exercise habit

Habit 3: SOCIAL ENERGY (Here's One to Protect)

Oprah Winfrey, talk-show host, and owner of Harpo Studios meditates for 20 minutes every morning, shortly after waking up.

Meditation makes you more in-tune with yourself, how you feel, and how the world around you feels. It's great for focus, increased energy, decreased stress and lifts brain fog.[9]

The people around you have an impact on your energy levels. Successful people surround themselves with positive, go-getters – while the average person is drained by one or more toxic, or negative people in their lives. Social energy must be protected.

The third habit is – to meditate daily on how to optimize your social energy.

According to a Cigna Study, loneliness is at epidemic levels in America.[10] But this is never a good reason to allow anyone a place in your life.

[9] Sun, Carolyn, I Tried This Oprah Meditation Hack Every Day for Two Weeks. Here Are My 5 Takeaways, https://www.entrepreneur.com/article/310039

[10] New Cigna Study Reveals Loneliness at Epidemic Levels in America, https://www.prnewswire.com/news-releases/new-cigna-study-reveals-loneliness-at-epidemic-levels-in-america-300639747.html

Take a look at your connections and consider if they add, or take energy away from you as you meditate for 20 minutes every morning.

Extroverted, or introverted, you need the right kind of connections in your daily life. If you have energy vampires in your sphere, you must get rid of them to be at your best.

✓	Adopt positive social meditation

Habit 4: SELF-INVESTMENT (Knowing and Doing)

Albert Einstein believed in constant self-investment through learning, research and application of that newfound knowledge.

The day you stop learning, is the day you stop growing. And personal growth is what takes you towards income acceleration and success. Einstein knew that constant reading was critical to learning, but so was the application of the knowledge learned while reading.

He famously said that too much reading renders the brain lazy. To grow in his field, Einstein continued to study formally until he was 26, then pursued self-study. He was not, as many believe, a naturally talented genius savant – he studied, read and practiced knowledge.[11]

The fourth habit is – invest in your field of knowledge through reading and practice.

If you want to excel like Einstein, shift from consuming entertainment to consuming knowledge. This is easily done by dedicating an hour or more to

---

[11] Shead, Mark, Are You Reading Too Much?, http://www.productivity501.com/are-you-reading-too-much/8874/

reading and applying your newly discovered knowledge. Practice what you learn, to see the real difference.[12]

Carve an hour of your day, in the morning or evening to read a book and then realize its lessons. This can be split into 30 minutes of reading, 30 minutes of creating.

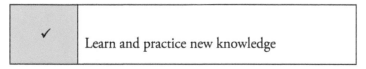

✓	Learn and practice new knowledge

Habit 5: DELEGATION (Focus on The Big Picture)

Richard Branson, Founder of Virgin and hundreds of other companies, is famous for his practice of 'letting go, to grow.' He delegates to focus on the big picture.13

Delegation is a habit that most people fail to practice. Instead, they try to do everything themselves and end up burned out, exhausted and depleted.

When you actively practice delegation, you become a talented multitasker, able to orchestrate and design your own career. It is at this point your income will inflate.

The fifth habit is – to practice delegation often and keep your eyes on the big picture.

Your career, or income goals, maybe the big picture for now. Knowing where you want to end up gives you clarity of purpose, and will help you assign what is not important to those around you. This must be done in all aspects of your life that consume your time.

---

[12] How Much Did Albert Einstein Study?, https://www.forbes.com/sites/quora/2017/12/28/how-much-did-albert-einstein-study/#1595adeb28bc
[13] Richard Branson: Why Delegation is Crucial for Success,
https://www.virgin.com/entrepreneur/richard-branson-why-delegation-crucial-success

This habit will kick in when someone makes demands on your time. Ask yourself if it contributes to your big picture. If it does not, find a creative way of delegating it to another human being. Make this a habit, and soon you will be surrounded by competent people.[14]

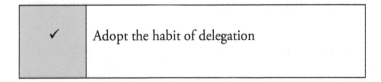

	Adopt the habit of delegation

Habit 6: MENTORING (Learning and Teaching)

Marie Forleo is a life coach, philanthropist and entrepreneur, who believes in the power of mentoring and being mentored, to become hugely successful.15

In fact, she uses connections to grow her business at every level. With storytelling and the ability to build a community around her lifestyle brand, she was named Oprah's *"thought leader for the next generation."*

Your ability to surround yourself with the right people will be the single most useful habit you can adopt. Most people never actively practice the art of conscious mentoring.

The sixth habit is – to practice attracting network connections that will help you excel!

Who do you know that could teach you something important? Have you ever met someone who you wanted to learn from? Teaching and learning is

---

[14] Coleman, Alison, Delegate Like Branson: Hire People Who are More Talented Than You, https://www.forbes.com/sites/alisoncoleman/2015/01/25/delegate-like-branson-hire-people-who-are-more-talented-than-you/#4ce10d27cb3d

[15] Brouwer, Allen, Lavery, Cathryn, Why Marie Forleo Says This One Marketing Trick Is So Important, https://www.entrepreneur.com/article/305586

fundamental to networking, and the basis for all positive relationships, in a corporate environment.[16]

Every day, you should consciously invest more energy in stimulating and improving mentor relationships that will help you grow and succeed as a person in your field. Be ruthlessly selective about your friends and who you spend the most time with.

Allow others to mentor you, and be mentored by you, in a working environment.

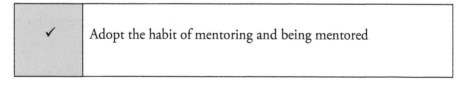

| ✓ | Adopt the habit of mentoring and being mentored |

Habit 7: YOUR 96 MINUTES (This is Your Most Valuable Time)

Stephen King is known for his work ethic and ability to produce six good pages of writing every day consistently. He does this by following the same productivity routine daily. 17

You need to have the discipline and consistency required, to do something for your direct productivity benefit, for 96 minutes a day. Why 96 minutes?

Science says that everyone has 96 highly productive minutes every day, a time window when you have the most energy and are at your best. If you harness this

---

[16] Forleo, Marie, Networking For Introverts W/Susan Cain,
https://www.marieforleo.com/2013/11/susan-cain-introverts-networking/
[17] Cotterill, Thomas, Stephen Kings Work Habits,
https://thomascotterill.wordpress.com/2012/09/13/stephen-kings-work-habits/

power and use it for your ultimate goal of earning more money, it shifts from possible, to probable.[18]

The seventh habit is – Spend 96 minutes a day working on your main career goal.

Discover when your 96 minutes kicks in. It might be just after waking up. It might be late at night when everyone else is sleeping. Find your window and use it.

Spend those 96 minutes focused exclusively on your main career goal. If that is to get a promotion, this is when you will plan and execute a strategy. If it is to launch a website, this is when you will put in the work.

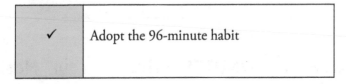

✓	Adopt the 96-minute habit

Habit 8: INNOVATION (Get to The Core of Things)

Elon Musk, the founder of PayPal, SpaceX and Tesla, is a known innovator and practices the Richard Feynman technique mixed with first principles, to stay creative. 19

The underlying concept of this technique is to not try and remember, but to understand – because when you do, you automatically remember. It's a way to entertain new ideas and be creative in a way that promotes productivity.

Knowledge to Elon, is about understanding the fundamental principles of a thing, to know the trunk and branches before diving headlong into the details, or the leaves of an idea.

---

[18] The Rule of 96 Minutes to Productivity, http://sapience.net/blog/the-rule-of-96-minutes-to-productivity/
[19] The Feynman Technique: The Best Way to Learn Anything, https://fs.blog/2012/04/learn-anything-faster-with-the-feynman-technique/

The eighth habit is – when learning something new, to understand its core first.

Applying this to your career will make you a forward-thinking innovator. For example, if you are a psychologist, you would benefit from learning more about neuroscience, because it is at the core of your field. Competency is all about strong, unshakable fundamentals.[20]

Spend 30 minutes every day learning something that reinforces how you innovate in your chosen field. Soon you will be questioning, brainstorming and seeing patterns that may amount to improvements you can implement.

✓	Practice innovation for 30 mins a day

Habit 9: THE WIN-WIN (Mutually Beneficial Relationships)

Stephen Covey, author of the smash hit "The 7 Habits of Highly Effective People" advocated the importance of win-win relationships.

According to Covey, most people approach life with a scarcity mindset, as opposed to an abundance mindset. Because of this, social interactions become unbalanced.[21]

There are several types of human interaction, win-lose, lose-lose, lose-win – but none are as powerful or effective as the win-win. When you practice win-win

[20] Stillman, Jessica, 3 Smart Strategies Genuises Like Albert Einstein and Elon Musk Use to Learn Anything Faster, http://www.businessinsider.com/3-strategies-geniuses-like-elon-musk-use-to-learn-anything-faster-2017-10?IR=T

[21] Hussain, Anum, 7 Habits of Highly Effective People [Book Summary], https://blog.hubspot.com/sales/habits-of-highly-effective-people-summary

interactions, your engagements are mutually beneficial, and people will enjoy working with you.

The ninth habit is – to practice win-win human interactions in your daily life.

When you do, you will find that people flock to you, because they see the benefits of doing business with you. When everyone benefits, you can succeed together.

This habit will cue when someone asks you for something. This should be your trigger to think about how you can make the interaction a win-win scenario. Covey says, to take consideration and courage into account, and to be creative in your problem-solving.

As you create win-win results, your influence will grow in your field. Remember that there is enough success around for everyone, and you can create it for them!

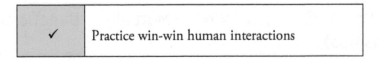

| ✓ | Practice win-win human interactions |

Habit 10: SPEAK UP (Know and Communicate Your Value)

Tyra Banks, ex-supermodel, TV producer and personality, based her career success on the ability to speak up, negotiate and get what she desires most.

She made a habit of speaking clearly, frankly and openly about her value with the people around her. Too often, we get stuck in the habit of remaining passive, and silent about our worth. Promotions and opportunities will pass you by because you failed to speak up.

The tenth habit is – to speak up when necessary about your value as an employee.

Tyra explains, that it is a shift from an 'I need' to an 'I deserve' mindset. Instead of explaining to your employer why you need a raise, you should explain why you deserve one. This is easily done by focusing on your value – or how you positively contribute to the company.[22]

This is another habit that will cue when you identify opportunities or feel that you deserve a promotion at your job. In meetings, be open about your contributions to the success of projects or initiatives. Speak up about how you, as a person, make things better.

Getting into the habit of communicating your worth to people around you, positions you for rapid advancement. If you cannot see and communicate your value, the higher-ups will not see it either. Be persistent. Have a clear voice. And do not get lost in the crowd.

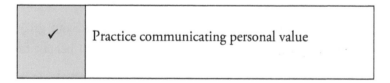

✓	Practice communicating personal value

Habit 11: PAY YOURSELF FIRST (This is Ground-breaking Advice)

George Clason was the author who wrote the classic 'The Richest Man in Babylon' and taught people to pay themselves first, in order to gain real wealth.23

---

[22] Atalla, Jen, Tyra Banks on How to Ask for a Raise,
http://www.businessinsider.com/tyra-banks-how-to-ask-for-a-raise-2018-4?IR=T
[23] Canfield, Jack, The Key to Wealth: Pay Yourself First,
http://jackcanfield.com/blog/the-key-to-wealth-pay-yourself-first/

Imagine if, since you had started working at age 21, you had put away 10% of every paycheck. This is what it means to pay yourself first. Money saved and kept earns compound interest and grows exponentially over long periods of time.

People that want to be wealthy use this strategy to move from employed earning to investing. Investing money is how you break out of your income bracket altogether.

The eleventh habit is – to put 10% of every paycheck aside to grow your wealth.

It might seem like very little at first, but 5 years of putting away just $100.00, frees up $6000.00 for investment. It gives you options to supplement your salary as you age.

To start the habit, every time you are paid – immediately take 10% of that total amount and put it in a separate account. You cannot touch this money. It is there simply to exist and earn you money from long-term growth.

The pay yourself first habit will help you clear away your debt, and get you investing at a young age. Get into this habit early, and you will benefit from time itself.

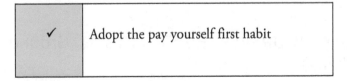

✓	Adopt the pay yourself first habit

Habit 12: SIDE HUSTLE (Spend Your Time for Returns)

Rob Kalin never meant Etsy.com to be such a smash success. Initially, it was simply his side hustle, born from a desire to make wood-encased computers. 24

Rob Kalin is a furniture designer who started Etsy as a place to sell his wares. It was a side hustle, an increasingly common play among Millennials. Some 61% of Millennials work on their side hustles once a week or more.[25]

This is usually a job that earns them money beyond their 9-5, or a personal project with income potential that they are developing. What is your side hustle?

The twelfth habit is – work on your side hustle twice a week.

On Mondays and Thursdays, or Tuesdays and Fridays you should dedicate a couple of hours to your side hustle. This is a second business, born from your creative or analytical talents that may become a solid earner for you down the line.

Scheduling in time to develop your secondary projects is important for personal growth, and increasing your income. Many Millennials discover that once their side businesses reach a certain level, they can either sell them or commit fulltime to their passions.

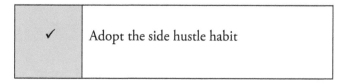

✓	Adopt the side hustle habit

---

[24] Green, Penelope, Scratching an Itch, https://www.nytimes.com/2016/05/05/style/etsy-rob-kalin.html

[25] Sophy, Joshua, More Than 1 in 4 Millennials Work a Side Hustle, https://smallbiztrends.com/2017/07/millennial-side-hustle-statistics.html

Habit 13: SUNDAY REVIEW (3 Hours to Financial Freedom!)

Suze Orman, a personal finance expert and personality, is known for teaching people to pick just one thing about their finances to work on, at a time. 26

She called it the 'one and done' method, and it simplifies the huge challenge of getting hold of your financial situation. Many people find their finances overwhelming, and so never take proactive steps towards understanding and controlling them.

The thirteenth habit is – to spend 3 hours every Sunday focusing on one financial problem.

You might need to save, or clear debt, or better understand your expenses and how to curb them. Whatever you need, you will tackle it during a designated time, every Sunday.

When you practice the habit of reviewing your finances regularly, to better understand and control them, you will change your life.

Make sure that you pick only one simple thing at a time so that you can properly digest and institute changes as necessary. Spend the time learning and streamlining for your ultimate benefit, as a responsible financial planner.

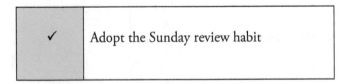

✓	Adopt the Sunday review habit

---

26 Financial Resolutions for 2017? Just Do This One Thing,
https://www.suzeorman.com/blog/financial-resolutions-for-2017-just-do-this-one-thing

Habit 14: MINIMALISM (Know How to Spend)

Steve Jobs, Founder of Apple, was a noted minimalist and wore the same black turtleneck every day for many, many years.

Popularized by Silicon Valley, minimalism reduces decision-fatigue, a common problem in today's overcrowded, ultra-informed society. With so much information and choice out there, it is no wonder you struggle to make good decisions for yourself.[27]

The theory goes that you can only make so many strong decisions in a day. The minimalist habit, allows you to dedicate those decisions to things that matter, like spending for value.

The fourteenth habit is – to spend with minimalism in mind.

Consumer culture is not for the truly rich. Instead, these individuals spend more money on a single item of quality, than repeated spending on numerous low-quality items.

Get into the habit of spending money on quality items, instead of cheaper items that will wear and degrade. This will free up your time as you make fewer wardrobe decisions. Instead of spending your creative energy there, you will spend it at work, where it matters most.

Less items of higher quality will simplify and improve your life.

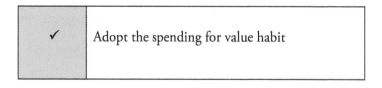

✓	Adopt the spending for value habit

---

[27] Steve Jobs and Minimalism, http://www.applegazette.com/ipod/steve-jobs-and-minimalism/

SECTION 4: THE GOLDEN RULE OF SUCCESS SEQUENCING

Your habits determine your behavior, but one thing is more important.

Focus.

Your attention is a form of currency that will either enrich or impoverish your life. That is why they call it 'paying attention.' Focus is the literal gateway to learning, reasoning, decision-making, problem-solving and perception.[28]

That is why consistent focus on your habits is the golden rule of success.

None of the people you have read about in this guide could have succeeded without an all-encompassing focus on their daily habits. Every individual here keeps a rigorous, personalized schedule that optimizes these habits.

Success, like your daily habits, is incredibly personal. Only you can decide when you have achieved a high enough level of success. And your habits are the stepping stones!

If you want to double your income, nothing is keeping you from it, but your habits. When you remove the bad and replace it with these powerful income-generating habits, you will immediately experience rapid change that will reshape your life.

That is why your primary focus must be a habitual practice, according to a personalized schedule. Without it, expect to fall back into bad patterns of behavior.

---

[28] Dr Taylor, Jim, Focus is The Gateway to Business Success, https://www.huffingtonpost.com/dr-jim-taylor/focus-is-the-gateway-to-b_b_4206552.html

SECTION 5: THESE HABITS WILL MATTER MOST!

According to a study from Northwestern University, a domino effect happens when you adopt one lasting good habit.[29]

In other words, exercising every day will encourage positive eating habits. In turn, this may spread to you getting better quality sleep and performing better at work. Management of these small, seemingly insignificant habits starts with internalizing just one.

I want you to pick a habit from this list to act as your linchpin habit.

Then I want you to dedicate the next 66 days to internalizing that habit, and when you feel capable, adopt more from this list.

Even if you struggle to adopt more of these habits, I want you to commit to just the one. At no point over the next 66 days will you, at any point, stop practicing that habit.

The first couple in this list have the most impact. They directly affect your daily performance. This is how you will naturally double your income in the short term.

Consider the domino effect active in you right now. But it is focused on negative habits. Switch to replacing them with positive habits, and you will soar!

The habits that matter most are the ones you learn to keep. Make them part of who you are, and soon you will leap an income bracket.

---

[29] Clear, James, How to Create a Chain Reaction of Good Habits, https://jamesclear.com/domino-effect

SECTION 6: WILLPOWER OR WONTPOWER: YOU DECIDE

The number 1 barrier to change is a mysterious thing called 'willpower.'

Those who have it are strong. Those who lack willpower are weak.

That is what we are taught to believe in our modern society. Your ability to resist short-term temptations is chalked up to your measure of willpower.

But you are never told what it is, or how to get it. How is it meant to take over, when you have no idea how it works?

Now I am going to lift the veil.

Willpower is little more than self-control. It is the conscious act of choosing what is right, over what is easy. It is picking cognition, over emotion. It is discipline.[30]

Willpower is a *habit*.

Right now, you habitually give in to your desires. What you need to do is replace this with your long-term plan for success. Say no to instant gratification!

Practice consciously choosing to focus on what is most important, every day.

If you don't want to exercise, use your willpower. Emotions drive your thoughts. Replace them with conscious thoughts that are more beneficial. You must exercise, to feel good today, tomorrow, this week. You must exercise to earn more and be better.

Practice willpower as a habit, and soon it will take over.

---

[30] What You Need to Know About Willpower: The Psychological Science of Self-Control, http://www.apa.org/helpcenter/willpower.aspx

SECTION 7: REGAINING YOUR FAITH IN FREE WILL

'But I have so much to do.'

'I'll begin after my major project is over.'

'I'll just let this week pass, and I'll be ready.'

It is human nature to wait for the ideal time to change. You might have bought this guide with the intent to adopt these habits 'at some point.'

This is because you have lost faith in free will. Free will is your ability to choose between different courses of action, unimpeded. Now, life is all about impediments, but that does not mean you cannot choose to be better. You can.

We are all made up of a unique blend of strengths, weaknesses, circumstances and perceptions. Your free will must be exercised in accordance with your make-up, within your unique context, under your special circumstances.

The price of freedom is struggling.

The price of earning more is learning to be better.[31]

Then being better – every day!

If you cannot be better consistently, hope is lost.

In this way, free will gives you the opportunity to be whoever you want, as long as you are willing to go through the wringer to get there. It will be hard! If it were easy, everyone would be successful and living these rare lives.

My advice to be something is to practice.

Start and start *today*.

---

[31] Dr Schwartz, Seth, Do We Have Free Will,
https://www.psychologytoday.com/us/blog/proceed-your-own-risk/201311/do-we-have-free-will

Check Out Our Other AMAZING Books:

1. *Resolving Anxiety and Panic Attacks*

A Guide to Overcoming Severe Anxiety, Controlling Panic Attacks and Reclaiming Your Life Again

Worldwide, one in six people is affected by a mental health disorder. So you are not alone in this (Ritchie & Roser, 2019). There is a difference between clinical anxiety and everyday anxiety. Everyday anxiety is normal and in often cases, it is necessary, while chronic anxiety will leave you functionally impaired. This book will not only inform you about anxiety and panic attacks but also introduce you to various methods and techniques that aid in getting rid of anxiety. It is a perfect package if you want to make long-lasting, meaningful changes in your life in a way that gets rid of anxiety. Knowledge is power, so gaining information about anxiety and panic attacks already puts you in the lead against them.

In the first chapter, we'll start with the basic knowledge of panic attacks and anxiety. The symptoms of both are pretty much the same, but there are some major differences as well. Knowing their difference and similarities can help you clearly understand your condition. Some basic ways of coping with them are also explained alongside their symptoms.

After gaining knowledge about anxiety and panic attacks in the first section, you will seek answers and ways to overcome them. The second chapter goes more in detail about the physical effects of anxiety. There are some types of anxiety which are also talked briefly about in the chapter. There are also therapies and treatments that are used to overcome and control anxiety. Their details are discussed in the chapter from where you can figure out what sort of treatment will suit you better. Some other ways of coping with anxiety are also discussed and they will surely prove beneficial to the reader.

The third chapter will make you aware of how interrelated physical and mental healths are. There are also details on how to improve one's physical health to influence a person's anxiety positively. You will also learn how important practicing well-being is. If you are to ignore physical health, it will cause problems for your mental health as well.

The fourth chapter will delve deep into mindfulness and its vast benefits. Mindfulness is a very powerful tool we have but don't know how to use. It can be practiced through meditation techniques, etc. It makes us see things more clearly than ever before. Practicing Mindfulness will arm you against any anxiety and panic attacks. In this chapter, it is explained in detail what it means and what are its advantages.

In the fifth chapter, we will learn about meditation and how can it help manage anxiety. We first start off by knowing what it is. You also have got to know its benefits and various techniques from which one can pick according to their choice. We will also learn the accurate posture you should have during meditation. We will learn how mediation reinforces our brain to stave off anxiety and panic attacks. It is a long road but a successful one for sure. Besides helping us out with anxiety and panic disorder, meditation has numerous other benefits for our body and mind.

The sixth chapter will explore the meaning behind self-love and its importance in fighting anxiety. Our battle with anxiety has to start from a positive ground. We first have to be fully comfortable and respectful towards ourselves. You will also find out how lack of self-love can actually breed anxiety.

Opening about anxiety is not an easy task but could be very helpful against anxiety. How to go about the whole process is talked about in detail in the seventh chapter. You will also learn how to evaluate your therapist and choose the right one. In this chapter, there are also guidelines for people who have just recently become aware of their anxiety and now they want to seek help. It will give them knowledge about things to consider when talking to someone about mental health, what you should accept and be prepared for. There is also information about talk therapy there.

In the eighth chapter, we address the misunderstanding about anxiety. Despite affecting so many people, it remains a different experience for all of them. There are also common mistakes pointed out in that chapter which we'll go into detail the mistakes that make our anxiety worse.

The ninth chapter is about where we talk about putting our foot down and start to incorporate practices into our life which will help you get rid of anxiety and panic attacks. We will learn how to manage our responses. It is basically a comprehensive listing of all the things you should be avoiding or adapting to lead a healthy lifestyle free of anxiety.

Want to read more? Purchase our book on Anxiety and Panic Attacks today!

2. Cognitive Behavioral Therapy

How CBT Can Be Used to Rewire Your Brain, Stop Anxiety, and Overcome Depression

Cognitive stems from cognition, which encapsulates the idea of how we learn and the knowledge that we carry. The things you learn are part of your cognition, and what you do with that information is included in that category as well. Cognition includes a wide list of information that you might not fully realize.

Behavior is what we do. It is how we act. The things that you choose to say to other people are all about your behavior. How you react to what others have to say will exhibit your behavior as well. Your behavior is all about your mind interacting with your body and how that interacts with the people and other things that surround you.

Therapy is any form of help, usually from a trained professional, to help improve on whatever the therapy is specified for. You might get physical therapy to help regain strength in your knee after having a serious surgery. You can also get therapy to help overcome an alcohol or drug addiction.

Throughout this book, we're going to give you the basis you need to start understanding cognitive behavioral therapy. The three together—cognitive, behavioral, therapy—all make up CBT, which is a method that is going to directly help you overcome the mental illness that you are hoping to treat.

Therapy can be expensive, and even if you do have the means to go through with this process, you might struggle to find the right therapist. Sometimes, you might live in an area where there is only one therapist within a close distance, but you don't have a vibe with them that you find to be helpful. You might also find that you are desperate for help and that you want a therapist, but insurance coverage isn't always good for this.

By reading this book, you'll be able to find the tools you need to help with overcoming your most challenging thoughts. We are going to take you through the steps to identify the root issues and come up with specific methods to get you through.

Want to read more? Purchase our book on Cognitive Behavioral Therapy today!

3. Effective Guide On How to Sleep Well Everyday

The Easy Method For Better Sleep, Insomnia And Chronic Sleep Problems

"A well spent day brings happy sleep." — Leonardo da Vinci

Are you experiencing the worst restless feeling? Has your doctor diagnosed you with insomnia, restlessness, sleeplessness? When the whole world around you seems to be in peaceful deep slumber, you are the one who is restless. No matter what term is used to describe it, the fact is that it is you who is actually going through insomnia, and nothing could feel worse than that.

So you drag yourself from bed in the morning feeling as earth, with its entire lock stock and barrel, has decided to perch on your head for the day. Yet you go through the motions of the day, though you barely manage to make it through the hours. By the early night, you fall on to bed hoping this night will be different because you're dead tired and nothing will keep you from sleeping like a log. It's 2.00 a.m. now, dawn is breaking through and there you are, still wide awake and ready to scream to the world because no matter how tired you are or how hard you have tried, you simply can't get to sleep.

While there are proven facts and evidence of the devastating effects of sleeping less, the investigations are still on to establish the exact nature of effects resulting from too much sleep. Some researchers argue that people who sleep much longer than necessarily have a higher death rate. Physical and mental conditions such as depression or socioeconomic status can also lead to excessive sleep. There are other researchers who argue that the human body will naturally restrain it from sleeping more hours than really necessary. However, with research still underway for concrete evidence of the effects of over sleeping the best path you can choose is to adopt a sleeping pattern somewhere in the middle. According to the National Sleep Foundation, this middle range falls between seven and eight hours of sleep during the night. Despite these statistics, the best way to ensure you receive sufficient sleeping time is to let your own body act as your guide. You can always sleep a little extra if you feel exhausted or sleep a little less than usual if you feel you are oversleeping.

Dangers of Sleep deprivation.

Though sleep is something the average human being takes for granted, it is also one of the greatest mysteries in life. Just like we still don't have all the answers to the quantum field or gravity, researchers are still exploring the reasons behind the 'whats' and 'whys' of sleep. However, one fact unchallenged about sleep is that a proper sleep is paramount for maintaining good health. The general guideline regarding the optimal amount of sleep for an adult range from six to eight hours! If you carry on with too little or too much of this general guideline you are exposing yourself to the risk of adverse health effects.

Though sleep is something that comes naturally to many people, the problems of sleep deprivation have today become a pressing problem with more and more people succumbing to chronic sleeping disorders. Unfortunately, a great number of these people do not even realize that lack of sleep or sleep deprivation is at the root of their manifold problems in life. Scientific research also points out that lack of sleep on a continuous scale can lead to severe repercussions on your health.

If you have been experiencing impaired sleep patterns for a longer period, you also face the risk of:

- Severely impairing your immunity strength

- Promoting the risk of tumor growth, as it has been scientifically established that a tumor can grow at least two to three times faster among animals subjected to severe sleeping dysfunctions within a laboratory setting.

- Creating a pre-diabetic condition in the body. Insomnia creates hunger, making you want to eat even when you have already had a meal. This situation can lead to problems of obesity in turn.

- Critically impairing memory. How many times during the day have you found it difficult to remember even the most mundane and repetitive events when you have had no more than 4 – 5 hours of sleep? Even a single night of impaired sleep plays havoc with our memory faculties, just think what it can do to your brain if you consistently lose sleep.

- Ruining your performance level both physically and mentally as your problem-solving abilities will not be working in peak order.

- Stomach ulcers

- Constipation, hemorrhoids

- Heart diseases

- Depression, lethargy and other mood disorders

- Daytime drowsiness

- Irritability

- Low energy

- Low mental clarity

- Reaction time slows down

- Lower productivity

- More accidents and mistakes

- Lower levels of growth hormone and testosterone

The growth hormone in the body which is vital for maintaining our looks, energy, and skin texture is produced by the pituitary gland. The specialty of this hormone production procedure is that it is only produced during the times of deep slumber or during intense workout sessions. In the absence of normal production of the growth hormone, our bodies will start on a premature aging process. According to research, people suffering from chronic insomnia are three times more susceptible to contract fatal diseases. When you lose sleep overnight, you cannot make up for it by sleeping more the next day. A night's lost sleep will be lost forever. More alarmingly if you continue to lose sleep regularly, they will create a cumulative negative effect that will disrupt your general health. All in all, sleeping deficiencies can effectively make your life miserable, as you already know.

How Much Sleep Do I Really Need?

This is a question that remains a mystery just like the questions of why and what makes us want to sleep. In response to a question of how many hours of sleep do we really need, an expert has answered that it is actually lot less than what we have been taught. On the other hand, though a good night's sleep is vital for good health, overdoing the sleeping can be equally bad for us. But if you sleep less and continue this for too long, the result will be confusion between body and brain signals, resulting in muddled thoughts, lethargic feelings, and overall lassitude. So, the question remains, how many hours of sleep do we really need? Is it essential to sleep the prescribed number of eight hours a day or is catching up a good sleep on a five to six-hour basis enough?

The eight hours of sleep theory is increasingly becoming unpractical in this fast-paced lifestyle. Actually, the recommendation of eight hours of sleep arises based on the idea that our ancestors had their beauty sleep between 8-9 hours in the past. In today's context, this concept is regarded more or less as a myth. In a study conducted by the Sleep Research Center, youngsters within the age group of 8 to 17 generally sleep for about nine hours during the night. However, in the case of adults, this theory is not applicable as a majority of them are sleepless and many of them thrive after a solid sleep varying between 5-7 hours.

A research conducted by the National Institute of Health has established that people who sleep soundly for nine hours a day or more are actually two times more vulnerable than those who sleep less in developing Parkinson's disease. A study report released by the Diabetes Care states that people claiming to sleep less than five hours or more than nine hours daily are the ones with the highest risk of attracting diabetes. In contrast, a large number of contemporary studies prove that people with sleeping patterns that do not exceed or fall beyond seven hours daily possess the highest survival rate. The persons who experience sleeping disorders and sleep less than 4.5 hours have the worst survival rate.

When ascertaining the correct number of hours you should sleep, the fact is that there is no magic number of hours. It will depend on a person to person basis as well as factors like age, activity, and performance level. For example, smaller children and teenagers require more sleep compared to adults. Your personal requirements will not be the same as your friend or colleague who is of the same age and gender as you. Because your sleep needs are unique and individual. According to the National Sleep Foundation, the difference of sleep requirements between two people of the same age, gender, and activity level is due to their basal sleep needs and sleep debt.

Your basal sleep need is the number of hours of sleep you typically need to engage in optimal performance levels. The sleep debt comprises of the accumulated number of hours of sleep you have lost as a result of poor sleeping habits, a recent sickness, social demands, environmental factors, etc. A healthy adult generally possesses a basal sleep need between seven and eight hours each night. If you have experienced sleeping difficulties and as a result accumulated a sleep debt you will find that your performance level is not up to its usual standard, even if you wake up after seven or eight hours of restful sleep. The symptoms will be most apparent during the times the circadian rhythm naturally alters like during mid-afternoon or overnight. One of the ways of easing out of an accumulated sleep debt situation is to get a few extra hours of sleep for a couple of nights until you regain your natural sleeping rhythm and vitality during the day.

Understand what Kind of a Sleeper Are You?

Sleep, dear reader, is the precious restorative that rights so many physical and mental wrongs. The elixir that transforms life and puts a spring in your step, a smile on your face, and the feeling that you can take care of everything that comes your way is sleep. Undervalued, ignored, and forgotten until you wake up to the realization that it's one of the essential foundations of daily wellbeing.

So what kind of a sleeper are you? There are many studies and descriptions of how we sleep but the common consensus settles for the following five simple categories:

1. Lively, healthy early risers!

These happy individuals usually get the sleep they need and rarely feel exhausted or fatigued. They are typically younger than the other groups, usually married or with a long-term partner, working full-time and definitely a morning person with no serious medical conditions.

2. Relaxed and retired seniors.

This is the oldest group in the survey with half of the sample being 65 or older. They sleep the most with an average of 7.3 hours per night compared to 6.8 across all groups. Sleep disorders are rare even though there is a significant proportion with at least one medical disorder.

3. Dozing drones.

These busy people are usually married/partnered and employed but they often work much longer than forty hours a week. Frequently working up to the hour when they go to bed, they get up early so they're always short of sleep and struggle to keep up with the daily pressures of life. Statistically, they'll feel tired or fatigued at least three days a week.

4. Galley slaves.

This group works the longest hours and often suffers from weight problems as well as an unhealthy reliance on caffeine to get through the day. Shift workers often fall into this group and there is also a marked tendency to be a night owl or evening person. They get the least amount of sleep and are more likely to take naps yet, surprisingly, this group often believes that, despite the state of their health, they are getting enough sleep.

5. Insomniacs.

Here is the largest proportion of night people and many of them quite rightly believe they have a sleep problem. About half of this group feel they get less sleep than they need and the same proportion admits to feeling tired, fatigued and lacking energy most of the time.

So, which of the five groups do you think you fit into?

If you're a happy member of Group One, your sleep should by definition be absolutely fine. Don't worry. We've got some really good ideas to share with you to keep you right on track and we'll even add some special extra features to your nightly rest routine to maximize the experience. If you're not in this group, our aim is to help you become a full-time member of the healthy, happy sleepers' association! Membership is for life.

Group Three represents too many tired, irritable, and generally inefficient individuals whose quality of life is impaired because they're too tired too often. Their work suffers because they rarely have sufficient rest to successfully assimilate the day's events. Their home life is degraded because work intrudes too often and they're just too tired to enjoy the pleasures and comfort of a life away from work. Feeling tired becomes their default position and they know they need to do something to give their minds and bodies the rest they deserve. Individuals in this group frequently suffer from long- term mental, physical and emotional stress.

The fourth group is rightly described as the night owls. They work the longest hours and, as we noted above, they typically work shifts. The health problems associated with this group include a marked tendency towards obesity as well as a range of inflammatory diseases. Despite the fact that these people rarely look or feel well, they seem to ignore the evidence and usually claim to get enough sleep, relying on sugary energy drinks and caffeine to keep them awake during waking hours. They take naps because their bodies can't function without additional sleep during the day. An objective analysis of their health would typically reveal a range of health and wellbeing issues.

Insomniacs are the dominant members of Group Five, people who don't get enough sleep, can't get to sleep, and who know they have a problem. Unfortunately, many insomniacs end up taking prescription medication to deal with their symptoms and we have to question the benefits of this solution in light of the many unpleasant side effects associated with long-term sleeping pill dependency. For insomniacs, life is a constant struggle because of the accumulative effects of long-term sleep deprivation.

Health issues abound, depression becomes a major risk, their ability to function normally is often impaired, and they lose sight of their potential to deal successfully with life's daily challenges. They sometimes refer to their condition as living in a nightmare world where they are constantly exhausted and simply cannot function. It's completely understandable that a doctor would prescribe sleeping drugs because the dangers of sleep deprivation can be acute.

Before we begin to examine the practicalities of sleep, we need to know how much sleep is appropriate for each of us as individuals. It's not surprising that different age groups have different sleep requirements.

For example, very young children and infants can sleep in total for around 14 - 15 hours a day. And if you've got teenagers, you might have guessed that adolescents usually need more sleep than adults. Teens can easily sleep between 8.5 to 9.5 hours a night.

It's widely understood that during the first trimester, pregnant women often find they need a lot more sleep than usual. The fact is that if you feel tired during the day, find yourself yawning or taking a nap, you're short on sleep. And this is the time for you to do something practical, realistic, and effective to take care of the problem.

There are many myths surrounding the condition known as OAS or Obstructive Sleep Apnea. It's estimated that around 18 million Americans suffer from the condition but the numbers could be much higher because many people don't report the condition to their doctors. This condition is far more than just loud snoring, although snoring can be a sign of sleep apnea.

People with this condition skip breathing 400 times during the night. The delay in breathing can last from ten to thirty seconds and is then followed by a loud snore as breathing suddenly resumes. The normal sleep cycle is interrupted and this can leave sufferers feeling tired and exhausted during the day. It is a serious condition, especially since it can lead to accidents at work, problems when driving, as well as increasing the risk of heart attacks and strokes. It can affect people of all ages, including children, but tends to affect people more after the age of forty.

Weight also plays a part and there is evidence that shedding excess pounds can improve the condition. Despite all the advice and overwhelming evidence, there are still surprising numbers of sleep apnea sufferers who continue to smoke.

Smoking is a perfect way to increase the severity and risks of this debilitating condition.

If you've already trimmed your weight, quit smoking and tried sleeping on your side but still suffer from the condition, you need to see your doctor. There are many treatments available including a special mask that delivers constant air flow to keep the breathing passage open. Lifestyle choices can clearly make a positive difference, too.

Your body, your brain, your mind and your emotional functioning all rely on sufficient sleep to operate efficiently. If you don't get enough sleep, everything suffers. Research suggests that it's much harder than you might imagine to adapt having less sleep than your body needs. The sleep deficit has to be repaid at some point or we'll experience increasingly severe problems.

Simple techniques of preparing for bed

1. Try to get to bed early. The recharging of the body's adrenal system usually takes place between 11p.m. and 1a.m. in the morning. The gallbladder uses the same time to release the toxin build up in the body. If you happen to be awake when both these functions are taking place within your body, there is the possibility of the toxin backing up to the liver which can endanger your health very badly. Sleeping late are byproducts of modern living styles. However, the human body was created in synchronization of nature and its activities. That is why before the advent of electricity people used to go to bed just after sundown and wake up with sunrise.

2. Don't alter your bedtimes haphazardly. Try to stick to a pattern where you go to bed and wake up at the same time. This should be done even on weekends. The continuous pattern will help your body to fit into a rhythm.

3. Maintain a soothing bedtime routine. This can change from person to person. You can use deep breathing exercises, meditation, use of

aromatherapy, a gentle relaxing massage given by your partner, or even going through a complete and relaxing skin care routine. The secret is to get into a rhythm which makes you comfortable, relaxed, and ready for bed. Repeating it every day will help in easing out the tensions of the day.

4. Refrain from taking any heavy fluids two hours before bed time. This habit will minimize the number of times you need to visit the bathroom in the middle of the night. You should also make a habit of going to the bathroom just before you get into bed, so that you will not get the urge during night time.

5. Eat a meal enriched with proteins several hours before your bed time. The protein will enhance the production of L-tryptophan which is essential for the production of serotonin and melatonin. Follow up your meal with some fruit to help the tryptophan to cross easily across the blood brain barrier.

6. Refrain from taking any snacks while in bed or just before bed and reduce the level of sugar and grains in your dinner time as it will raise the blood sugar level, delaying sleep. When the body starts metabolizing these elements and the blood sugar level start dropping you will find yourself suddenly awake and unable to go back to sleep.

7. A hot bath before bed is found to be very soothing. When the body temperature is stimulated to a raised level during late evening by the time you get into bed, it will be ready to drop, signaling slumber time to your brain.

8. Stop your work and put them away ideally one to two hours before bed. The interval between work and bedtime should be used for unwinding from the pressure and tension of work. It is essential that you approach your bed with a calm mind instead of being hyped up about some matter.

9. If you prefer reading, a novel with an uplifting story instead of a stimulating one like suspense or mystery is recommended. Or the suspense will keep you up half the night awake trying to visualize the end to the mystery!

A Few Lifestyle Suggestions to Make You Sleep Better

Don't take medications and drugs unless it is absolutely necessary for your health and wellbeing. A majority of prescribed and over the counter drugs can cause changes in your sleeping patterns.

Avoid drinks with alcohol or caffeine. Caffeine takes longer to metabolize in the body so that your body will experience its effects much longer after consumption. That is why even the cup of coffee you had in the evening will keep you awake during the night. Some of the medications and drugs in the market also contain caffeine which account for their capacity to generate sleeping irregularities. Though alcohol can make you feel drowsy the effect is very much short lived. Once the feeling goes away, you will find that sleep is eluding you for many hours and even the sleep that you finally reach will not take you to deep slumber after alcohol. In the absence of deep sleep, your body will not be able to perform its usual healing and regeneration process is vital for lasting healthiness.

Engage in regular exercise activities. If you are contained in an 8-hour office job, you should make sure that your body receives plenty of exercise which can dramatically increase your sleep health. The best time to exercise is, however, not closer to your bedtime but in the morning.

Keep away from sensitive food types that will keep you awake at night like sugar, pasteurized dairy foods, and grains. These foods can result in congestion, leading to gastric disorders.

The sleep apnea risk is enhanced amongst people with weight issues. If you think you have gained a few extra pounds and during this time you have also experienced sleeping trouble focus on losing the extra weight as a priority. The sleeping issue will correct automatically.

If your body is going through a hormone upheaval like during menopausal or premenopausal time, seek advice from your family physician, as this time can lead to sleeping difficulties.

Want to read more? Purchase our book on Effective Guide On How to Sleep Well Everyday today!

Printed in June 2019
by Rotomail Italia S.p.A., Vignate (MI) - Italy